Mental Maths

LEVEL 3

MOONSTONE

Published in Moonstone
by Rupa Publications India Pvt. Ltd 2023
7/16, Ansari Road, Daryaganj
New Delhi 110002

Sales centres:
Allahabad Bengaluru Chennai
Hyderabad Jaipur Kathmandu
Kolkata Mumbai

P-ISBN: 978-93-5520-708-1
E-ISBN: 978-93-5520-709-8

First impression 2023

10 9 8 7 6 5 4 3 2 1

The moral right of the authors has been asserted.

Complete the place value chart below.

Hundred Thousands	Ten Thousands	Thousands			

Complete the place value chart with the given numbers.

Number	Thousands	Hundreds	Tens	Ones
6372	6	3	7	2
1227				
4843				
7954				
9000				
8530				

Write the numeral for the following number names:

One thousand four hundred and fifty six = 1,458

Six thousand nine hundred and twenty =

Two thousand five hundred and one =

Nine thousand six hundred and forty four =

Eight thousand eight hundred and eighty eight =

Five thousand and fifty six =

Write the number names for the following numbers:

7189 = Seven thousand one hundred and eighty nine

1248 =

8392 =

2039 =

5438 =

6736 =

Write the following numbers in expanded form:

7839 = | 7000 + 800 + 30 + 9 |

4325 =

1748 =

8345 =

2931 =

6432 =

Write the numbers in standard form.

3 thousands + 5 hundreds + 2 tens + 3 ones = | 3523 |

9 thousands + 0 hundreds + 1 tens + 4 ones =

4 thousands + 4 hundreds + 0 tens + 3 ones =

1 thousands + 5 hundreds + 0 tens + 6 ones =

7 thousands + 8 hundreds + 1 tens + 0 ones =

5 thousands + 2 hundreds + 8 tens + 8 ones =

Mention the place value of the following digits in the given numbers.

The place value of 6 in 7886 is  Ones

The place value of 1 in 4213 is

The place value of 5 in 1589 is

The place value of 9 in 8976 is

The place value of 4 in 4112 is

The place value of 0 in 8045 is

The place value of 2 in 5432 is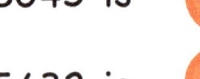

Fill in the blanks to complete the expanded form of the numbers.

8392 = __8__ thousands + __3__ hundreds + __9__ tens + __2__ ones

2237 = ____ thousands + ____ hundreds + ____ tens + ____ ones

4224 = ____ thousands + ____ hundreds + ____ tens + ____ ones

1548 = ____ thousands + ____ hundreds + ____ tens + ____ ones

2904 = ____ thousands + ____ hundreds + ____ tens + ____ ones

9400 = ____ thousands + ____ hundreds + ____ tens + ____ ones

6056 = ____ thousands + ____ hundreds + ____ tens + ____ ones

Fill in the blanks.

In 4821 the digit in thousands place is   4

In 9070, the digit in ones place is   _____

In 5876, the digit in hundreds place is   _____

In 6539, the digit in thousands place is   _____

In 8145, the digit in hundreds place is   _____

In 2212, the digit in ones place is   _____

In 2346, the digit in tens place is   _____

In 3227, the digit in hundreds place is   _____

In 5432, the digit in thousands place is   _____

In 1023, the digit in tens place is   _____

In 4386, the digit in ones place is   _____

In 2338, the digit in hundreds place is   _____

In 9024, the digit in thousands place is   _____

In 7647, the digit in tens place is   _____

In 4808, the digit in ones place is   _____

In 5302, the digit in hundreds place is   _____

In 1999, the digit in thousands place is   _____

In 6647, the digit in tens place is   _____

Exercise 6

Write the place values of the following digits:

In 9842, the digit 8 is in the __hundreds__ place.

In 8430, the digit 8 is in the _____ place.

In 1643, the digit 1 is in the _____ place.

In 2968, the digit 6 is in the _____ place.

In 4449, the digit 9 is in the _____ place.

In 6028, the digit 0 is in the _____ place.

In 4578, the digit 4 is in the _____ place.

In 6028, the digit 0 is in the _____ place.

Write the numbers in the standard form.

6 thousands + 1 hundreds + 0 tens + 2 ones = __6102__

4 thousands + 4 hundreds + 6 tens + 3 ones = _____

5 thousands + 1 hundreds + 1 tens + 7 ones = _____

9 thousands + 9 hundreds + 0 tens + 5 ones = _____

7 thousands + 0 hundreds + 2 tens + 2 ones = _____

2 thousands + 8 hundreds + 0 tens + 3 ones = _____

5 thousands + 3 hundreds + 1 tens + 1 ones = _____

8 thousands + 0 hundreds + 0 tens + 0 ones = _____

Regrouping

8 thousands + 14 hundreds + 15 tens + 4 ones
= 8 thousands + 10 hundreds + 4 hundreds + 10 tens + 5 tens + 4 ones
= 8 thousands + 1 thousand + 4 hundreds + 1 hundred + 5 tens + 4 ones
= 9 thousands + 5 hundreds + 5 tens + 4 ones

Regroup the following:

5 thousands + 7 hundreds + 12 tens + 2 ones = ____ thousands +
____ hundreds + ____ tens + ____ ones

2 thousands + 4 hundreds + 16 tens + 18 ones = ____ thousands +
____ hundreds + ____ tens + ____ ones

1 thousand + 18 hundreds + 15 tens + 2 ones = ____ thousands +
____ hundreds + ____ tens + ____ ones

4 thousands + 9 hundreds + 14 tens + 25 ones = ____ thousands +
____ hundreds + ____ tens + ____ ones

9 thousands + 1 hundreds + 2 tens + 75 ones = ____ thousands +
____ hundreds + ____ tens + ____ ones

2 thousands + 5 hundreds + 23 tens + 9 ones = ____ thousands +
____ hundreds + ____ tens + ____ ones

3 thousands + 0 hundreds + 15 tens + 2 ones = ____ thousands +
____ hundreds + ____ tens + ____ ones

7 thousands + 1 hundreds + 11 tens + 47 ones = ____ thousands +
____ hundreds + ____ tens + ____ ones

1 thousand + 3 hundreds + 14 tens + 31 ones = ____ thousands +
____ hundreds + ____ tens + ____ ones

6 thousands + 15 hundreds + 4 tens + 89 ones = ____ thousands +
____ hundreds + ____ tens + ____ ones

Exercise 8

Solve the following:

3543	3289	7383
+ 3245	+ 1234	+ 131
6788		

4332	1331	3882
+ 1646	+ 1221	+ 177

7388	1393	1564
+ 1646	+ 142	+ 1435

8399	4223	2839
+ 421	+ 1540	+ 3453

5482	7654	4332
+ 891	+ 2343	+ 3521

6755	5430	4455
+ 1320	+ 1121	+ 4310

Exercise 9

Fill in the empty boxes.

```
  42□3
+ 2513
──────
  6736
```

```
  6308
+ 2□00
──────
  8908
```

```
  241□
+ 1034
──────
  3449
```

```
  □105
+ 1130
──────
  3235
```

```
  11□1
+ 2528
──────
  3719
```

```
  8326
+ 164□
──────
  9968
```

```
  2643
+ 144□
──────
  4085
```

```
  □209
+ 6190
──────
  7399
```

```
  3201
+ 124□
──────
  4445
```

```
  1504
+ 1□04
──────
  2608
```

Exercise 10

Add and write the addition sentences.

A petrol pump sold 2020 l of petrol in a week and 3400 l of petrol in the next week. How many litres of petrol did it sell in the two weeks?

_____ + _____ = _____

Mr John counted the number of visitors to his shop. There were 5645 males and 3743 females. Find the total number of visitors.

_____ + _____ = _____

A farmer produced 6935 kg of wheat in the year 1999 and 4205 kg in 2000. Find the total production of wheat in two years.

_____ + _____ = _____

Tom is writing a novel. He wrote 3210 words on Monday and 1390 words on Tuesday. How many words did he write during these two days?

_____ + _____ = _____

Jojo drove 2980 m to a city. A week later, he drove 7462 m home. How many metres did he drive in all?

_____ + _____ = _____

Solve the following:

5643	4580	7383
− 1123	− 1934	− 2131
4520		

7832	5031	3532
− 3446	− 4221	− 1177

4238	9393	6433
− 4013	− 3142	− 5735

1453	5323	8939
− 1401	− 2340	− 5403

7482	6454	6392
− 2891	− 5641	− 2501

3755	9750	5435
− 2320	− 8125	− 1210

Fill in the empty boxes.

5598
− 2512
3076

9900
− 25☐0
7400

4326
− 154☐
2785

☐505
− 1402
5103

97☐2
− 9181
571

3890
− 12☐4
2656

5643
− 244☐
3199

☐584
− 3995
4589

541☐
− 2034
3376

7565
− 312☐
4445

Subtract and write the subtraction sentences.

A man bought 3476 tomatoes from a vegetable seller. Out of the total purchase, 1980 tomatoes were rotten. Find the number of good tomatoes.

_____ − _____ = _____

In a school library, there are a total of 9890 science books. If 4750 are only chemistry books, find the number of other science books.

_____ − _____ = _____

Kim sold 5649 litres of milk in the month of March and Tim sold 3865 litres of milk in the same month. How many more litres of milk did Kim sell?

_____ − _____ = _____

Peter's monthly salary is 3460 dollars, out of which he gives 1020 dollars to his wife for household expenses and deposits the rest in the bank. How much money does he deposit in the bank every month?

_____ − _____ = _____

An autoboigraphy has 2955 pages out of which 1050 pages are coloured. How many pages are printed black and white?

_____ − _____ = _____

Fill in the empty boxes to complete the addition sentences.

$2342 + \boxed{} = 8390$ $\qquad$ $\boxed{} + 7367 = 9999$

$3244 + \boxed{} = 5232$ $\qquad$ $5267 + \boxed{} = 8000$

$\boxed{} + 5637 = 6781$ $\qquad$ $\boxed{} + 2456 = 5378$

$\boxed{} + 1115 = 4352$ $\qquad$ $7368 + \boxed{} = 9893$

Fill in the empty boxes to complete the subtraction sentences.

$6666 - \boxed{} = 5555$ $\qquad$ $\boxed{} - 5221 = 1453$

$5322 - \boxed{} = 1000$ $\qquad$ $9489 - \boxed{} = 7488$

$\boxed{} - 4400 = 2431$ $\qquad$ $\boxed{} - 1435 = 4256$

$\boxed{} - 1252 = 4024$ $\qquad$ $8392 - \boxed{} = 3426$

Write the number that comes after:

4317 (4318)   7990 (   )

5452 (   )   3445 (   )

9864 (   )   2623 (   )

Write the number that comes before:

(1031) 1032   (   ) 9654

(   ) 6422   (   ) 3452

(   ) 7040   (   ) 1500

Write the number that comes in-between:

5678 (5679) 5680   1916 (   ) 1918

2229 (   ) 2231   9333 (   ) 9335

4478 (   ) 4480   7683 (   ) 7685

Exercise 16

More Than, Less Than

What is 526 more than 1465? | 1991 |

What is 999 more than 6320? | |

What is 834 more than 7349? | |

What is 231 more than 4234? | |

What is 743 more than 5003? | |

What is 810 more than 3600? | |

What is 240 less than 2045? | 1805 |

What is 985 less than 9378? | |

What is 226 less than 6742? | |

What is 515 less than 3753? | |

What is 837 less than 7489? | |

What is 189 less than 1555? | |

Exercise 17

Complete the number patterns.

3767	3768	3769	3770					3775	
					3782				

9031									
		9043						9049	

1886						1892			
				2000					

Count backwards and complete the number patterns.

4342							4335		
				4328					

7289						7283			
								7271	

2111									2102
	2100								

Continue the pattern by counting in 1000s.

Continue the pattern by counting in 1000s.

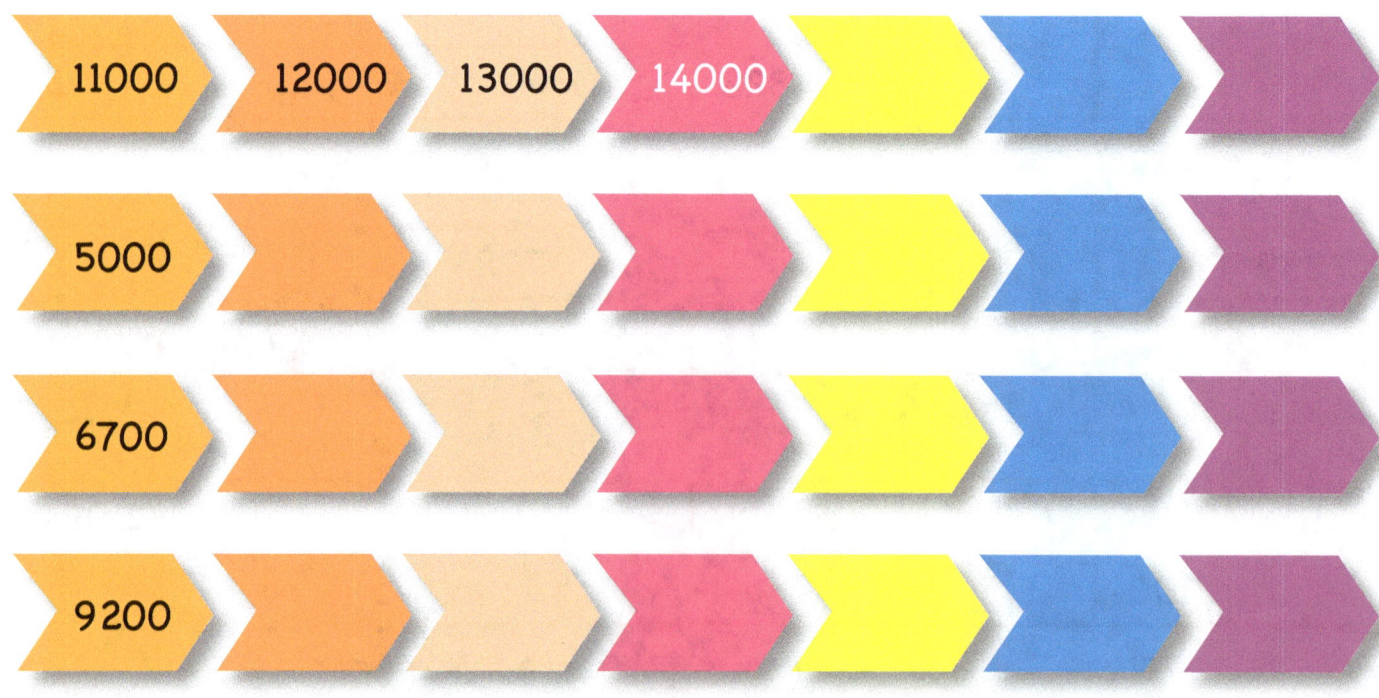

Exercise 19

Write the given numbers in ascending order.

6100, 2022, 7006, 1113, 4542	1113	2022	4542	6100	7006
1837, 1937, 1678, 1235, 1563					
2677, 4637, 9836, 5678, 1415					
8867, 1463, 3456, 9483, 4532					

Write the given numbers in descending order.

2321, 4534, 6743, 1975, 3241	6734	4534	3241	2321	1975
6743, 7859, 3427, 4000, 1435					
5500, 8977, 4537, 9479, 3426					
9479, 9102, 9678, 9000, 9999					

Exercise 20

Circle the biggest number among the given set of numbers.

9379, (9833), 9178, 9633, 9023

8483, 1119, 8646, 4448, 8643

7362, 9589, 2527, 5788, 1643

1533, 1589, 1527, 1508, 1520

6225, 8225, 1225, 4225, 7225

4242, 7543, 1234, 3423, 9653

Circle the smallest number among the given set of numbers.

(1011,) 3233, 8658, 1633, 4013

1233, 5419, 7656, 1118, 2243

7992, 9759, 4327, 8888, 7543

9643, 2210, 5627, 7548, 8823

6432, 1345, 6323, 2322, 7443

1254, 1454, 1154, 1054, 1354

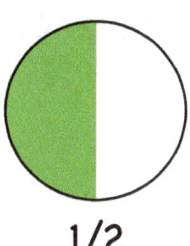

1/2

One-half

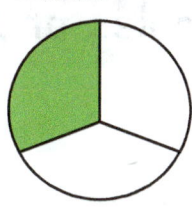

1/3

One-third

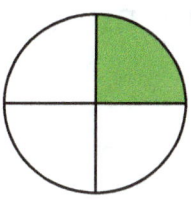

1/4

One-fourth

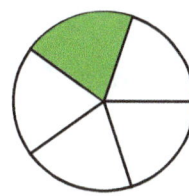

1/5

One-fifth

Write the fractions in the space provided below.

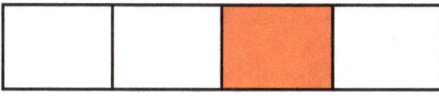

_____

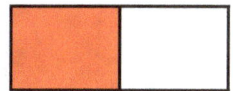

_____

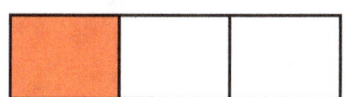

_____

_____

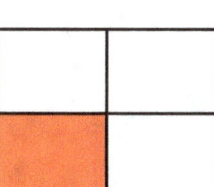

_____

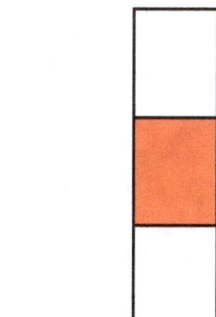

_____

Count and write the number of wholes and halves for each of the following:

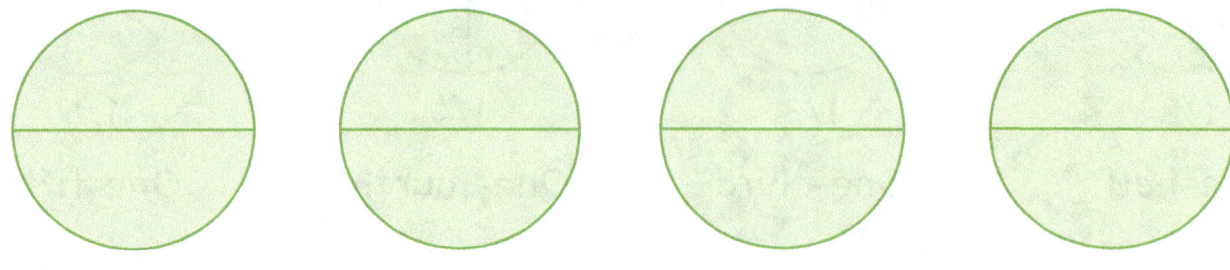

Wholes = _____4_____ and halves = ____8____

Wholes = _____ and halves = _____

Wholes = _____ and halves = _____

Wholes = _____ and halves = _____

Count and write the number of wholes and fourths for each of the following:

Wholes = ___3___ and fourths = ___12___

  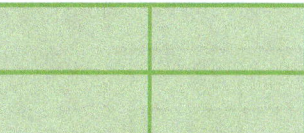 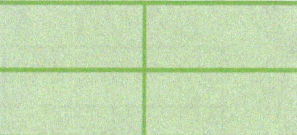

Wholes = _____ and fourths = _____

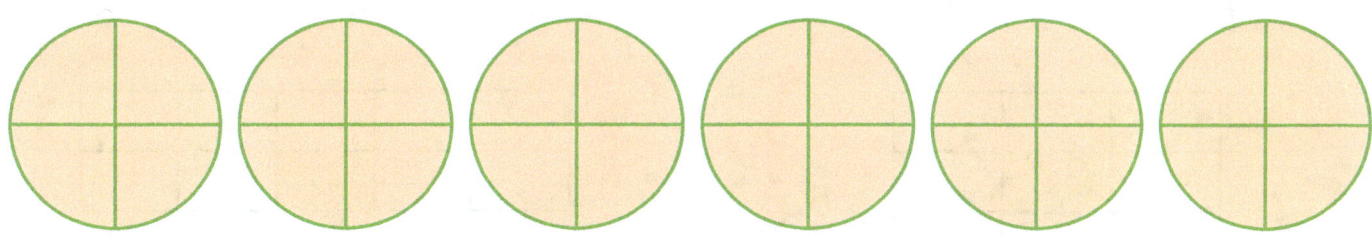

Wholes = _____ and fourths = _____

 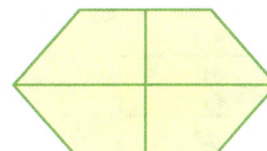 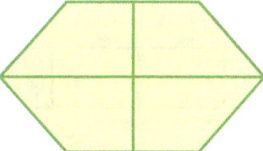

Wholes = _____ and fourths = _____

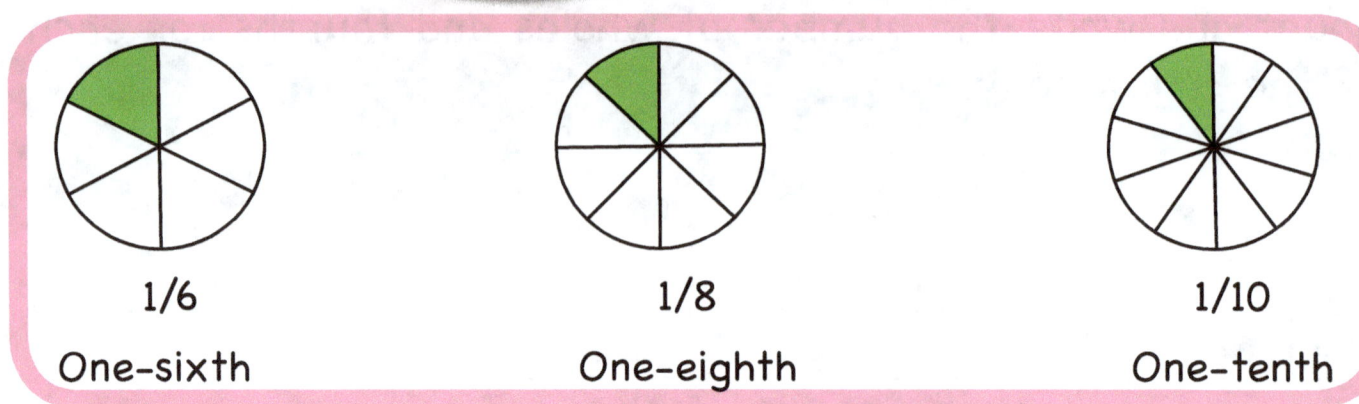

Exercise 24

1/6

One-sixth

1/8

One-eighth

1/10

One-tenth

Write the fractions in the space provided below.

____

____

____

____

____

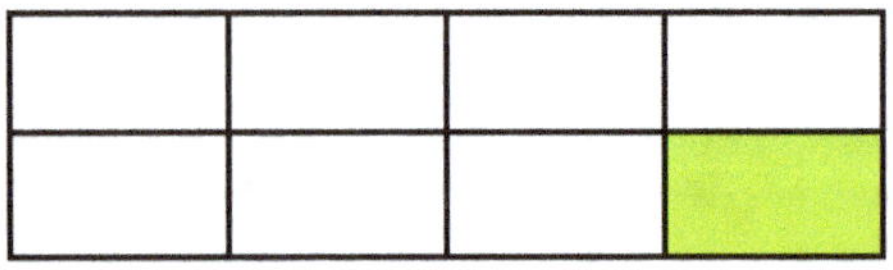

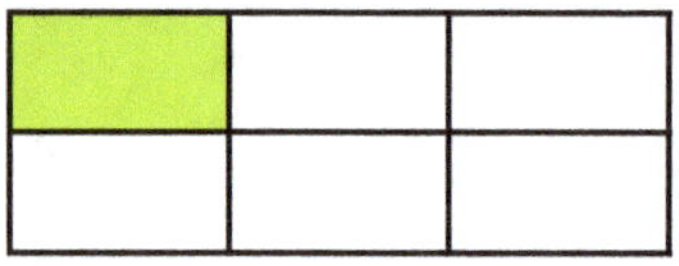

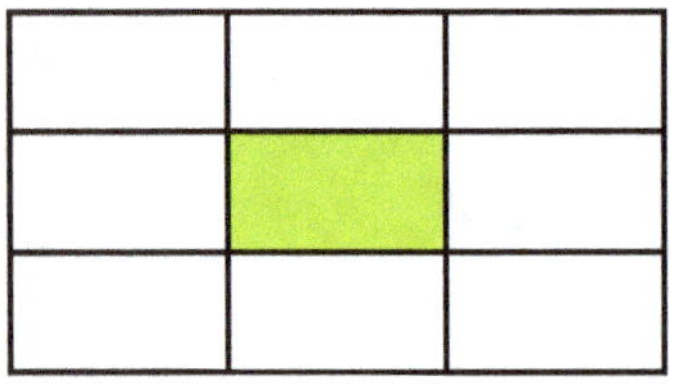

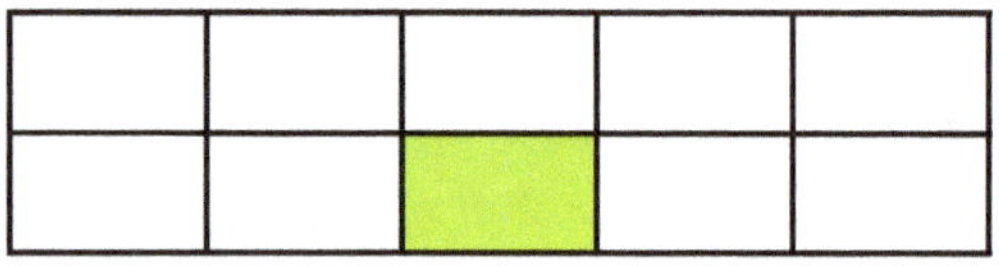

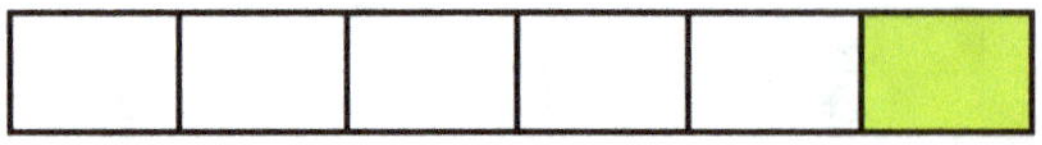

Draw and colour 1/2nd part of the following figures:

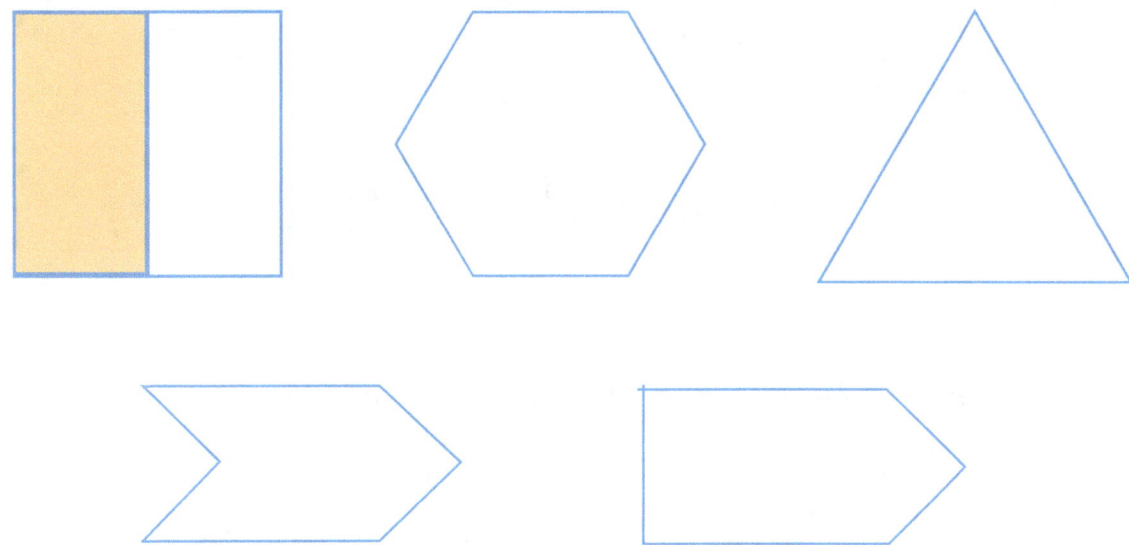

Draw and colour 1/4th part of the following figures:

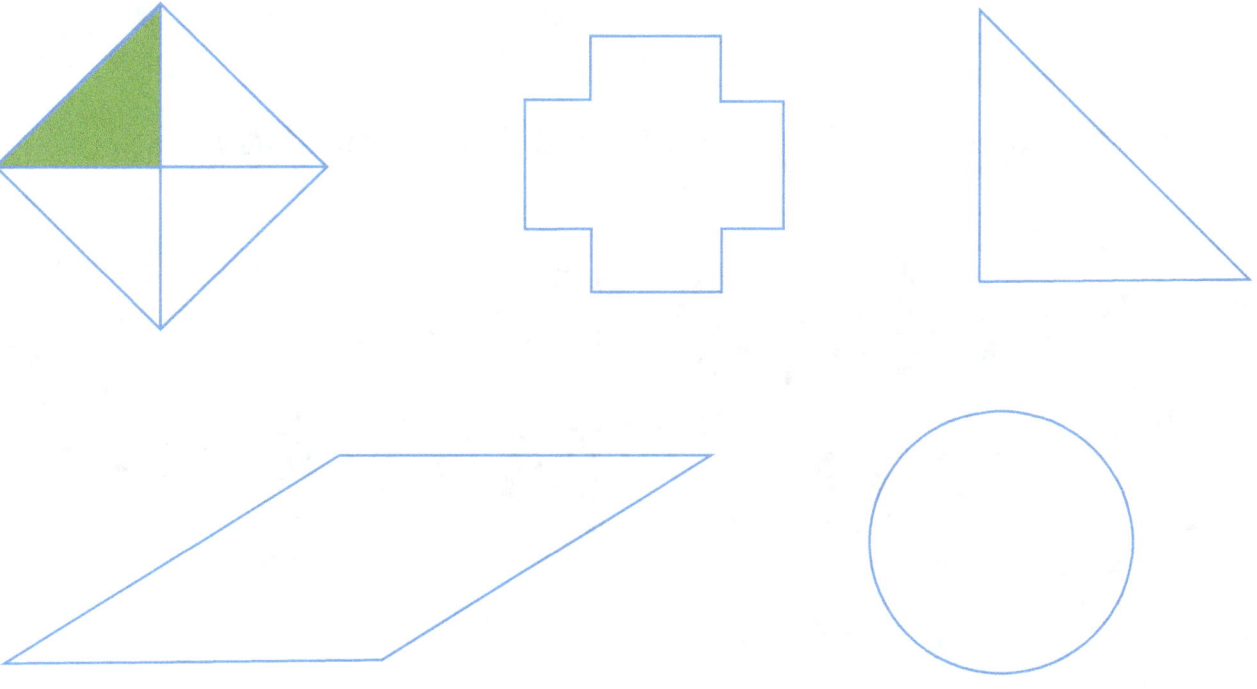

Draw and colour 1/5th part of the following figures:

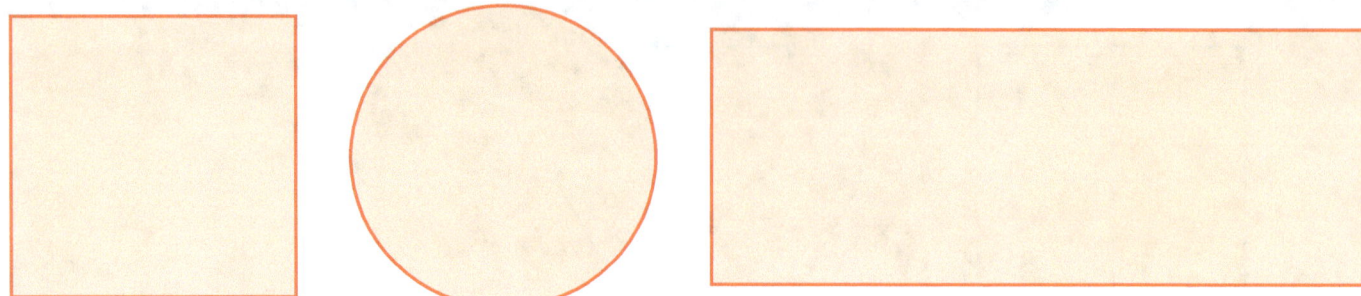

Draw and colour 1/6th part of the following figures:

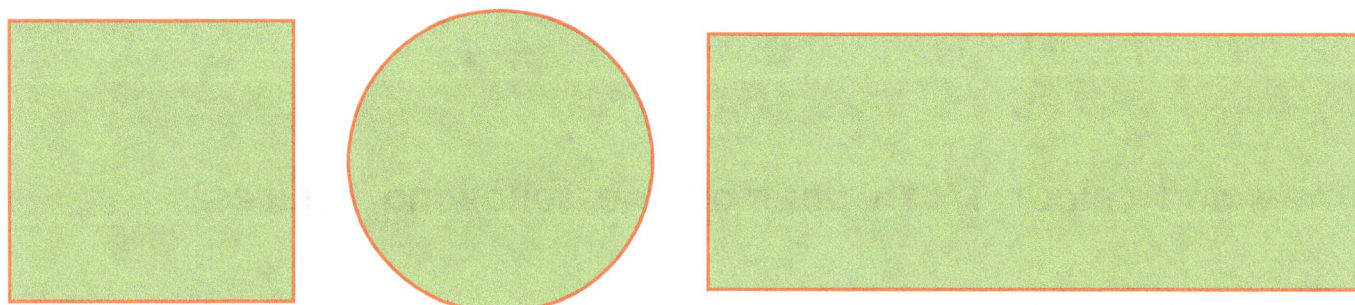

Draw and colour 1/8th part of the following figures:

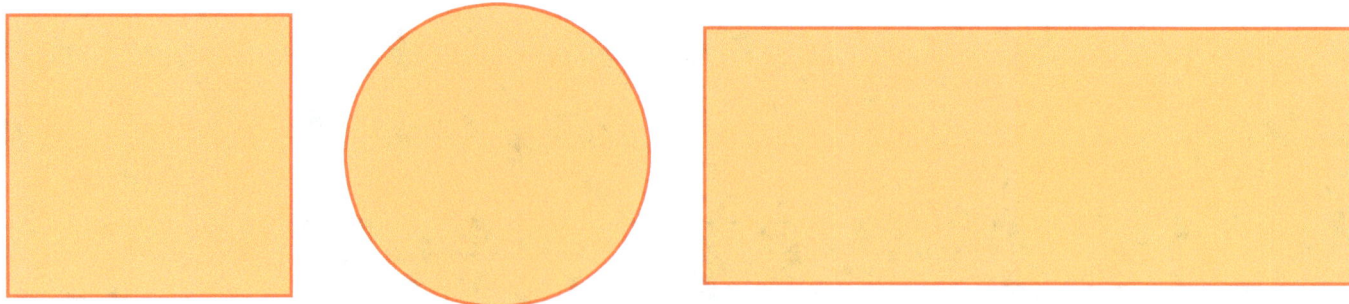

Count the number of parts and fill in the blanks accordingly.

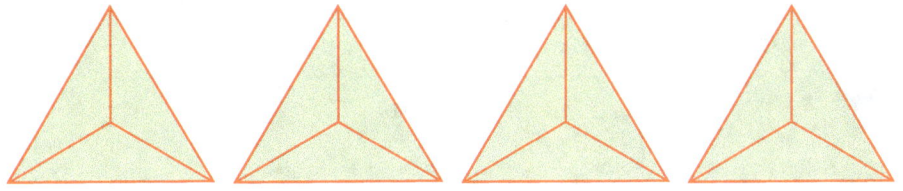

Wholes _____   Thirds _____

Wholes _____   Eighths _____

Wholes _____   Sixths _____

Wholes _____   Sevenths _____

Exercise 28

Colour the following diagrams to represent the given fractions:

1/5   1/3

1/6   1/2

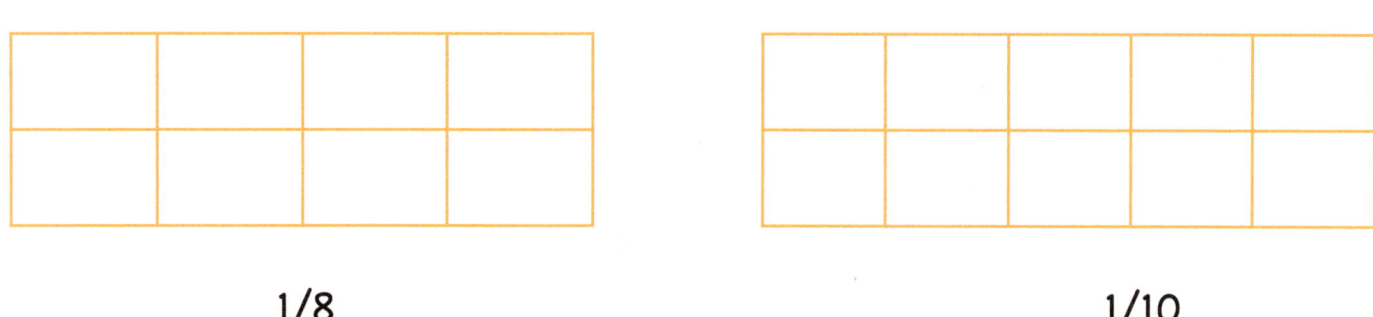

1/8   1/10

1/7   1/9

Study the diagrams given below and fill the blanks accordingly.

      represents 1/5 of a whole

      represents ____ of a whole

      represents ____ of a whole

      represents ____ of a whole

      represents ____ of a whole

      represents ____ of a whole

      represents ____ of a whole

      represents ____ of a whole

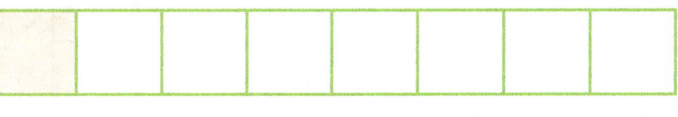
      represents ____ of a whole

      represents ____ of a whole

Exercise 30

Colour the following to represent the fractions.

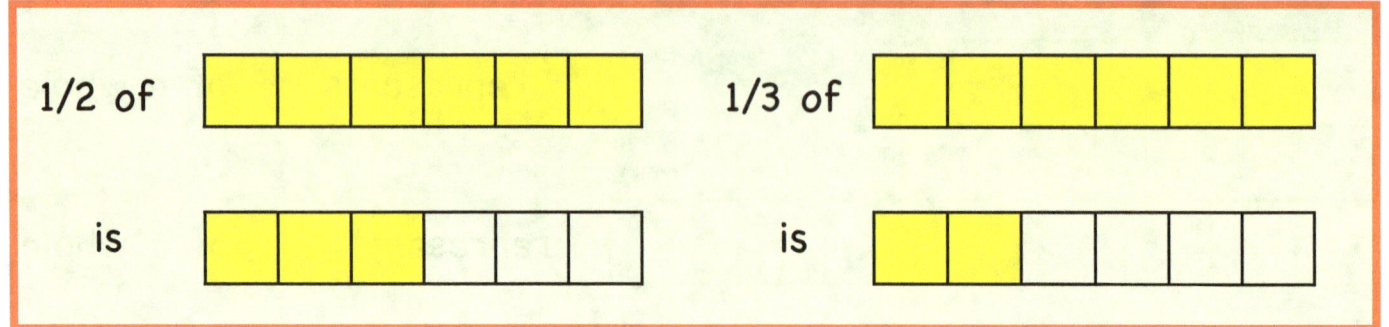

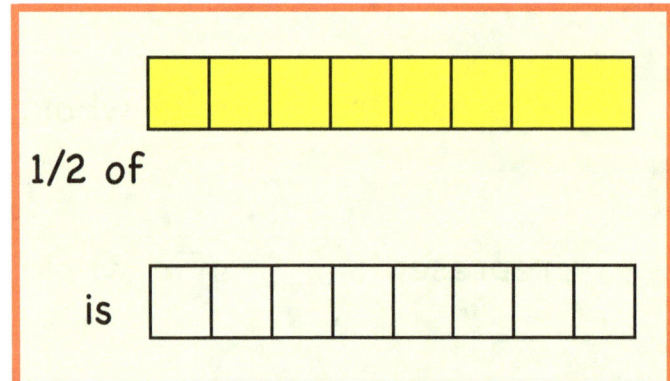

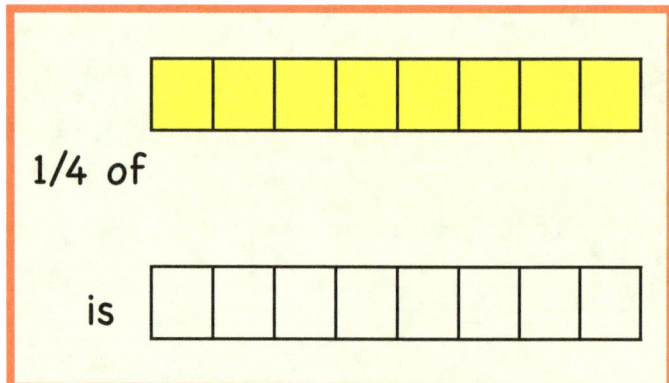

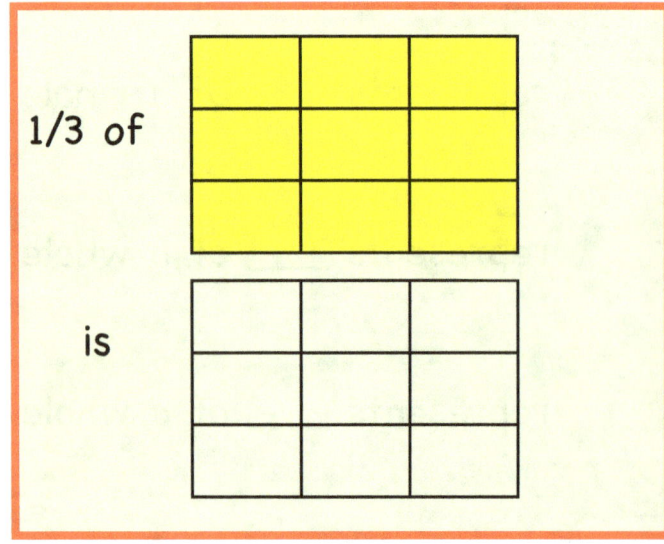

Fill in the blanks.

1/3 of  = (book)

1/3 of 3 books is 1 book

1/2 of 10 bananas are _____ bananas.

1/5 of 15 carrots are _____ carrots.

1/7 of 14 apples are _____ apples.

1/10 of 10 balls is _____ ball.

1/8 of 24 erasers are _____ erasers.

1/3 of 15 oranges are _____ oranges.

1/6 of 18 capsicums are _____ capsicums.

1/9 of 9 pencils is _____ pencil.

Solve the following:

1/5 × 10 = __2__   1/4 × 24 = _____

1/8 × 16 = _____   1/7 × 21 = _____

1/2 × 12 = _____   1/7 × 21 = _____

1/9 × 36 = _____   1/3 × 9 = _____

Answer the questions below.

How many halves will be there, if I cut each of the following fruits into two equal parts?

7 apples	4 oranges	10 peaches
14	_____	_____

How many fifths will be there, if I cut each of the following fruits into five equal parts?

3 apples	2 oranges	5 peaches
_____	_____	_____

How many eighths will be there, if I cut each of the following fruits into eight equal parts?

2 apples	1 orange	4 peaches
_____	_____	_____

How many tenths will be there, if I cut each of the following fruits into ten equal parts?

1 apple	4 oranges	6 peaches
_____	_____	_____

How many fourths will be there, if I cut each of the following fruits into four equal parts?

6 apples	4 oranges	5 peaches
_____	_____	_____

Which of the following figures represent one-fourth?

 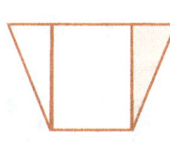 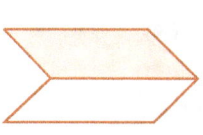 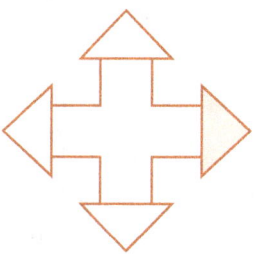

Which of the following figures represent half?

Which of the following figures represent one-third?

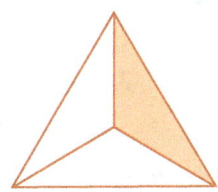  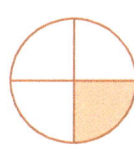 

Which of the following figures represent one-eighth?

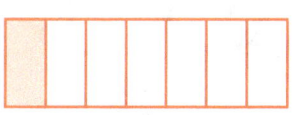   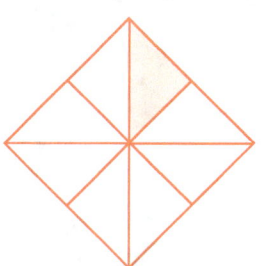

Exercise 34

Encircle the 1/4th part of the following sets:

 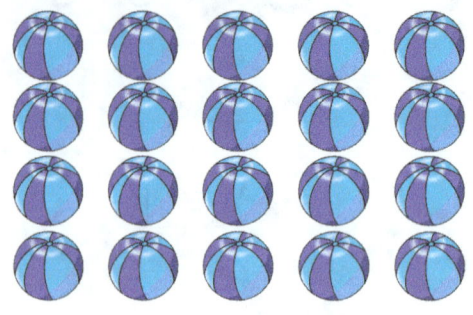

Encircle the 1/7th part of the following sets:

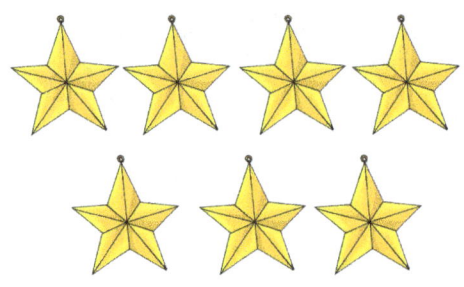 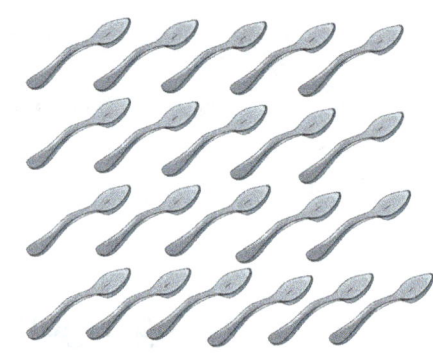

Encircle the 1/3rd part of the following sets:

Encircle the 1/5th part of the following sets:

| Fraction | ← | 1/5 = 2/10 = 0.2 | → | Decimal |
| Decimal | ← | 0.5 = 5/10 = 1/2 | → | Fraction |

Complete the following:

1/5 = ____/10 = 0.____

____/5 = 6/10 = 0.____

2/5 = ____/10 = 0.____

____/5 = 8/10 = 0.____

5/5 = ____/10 = _____

Convert the fractions into decimals.

1/4	=	_____	1/15	=	_____
1/8	=	_____	1/7	=	_____
1/10	=	_____	1/9	=	_____
1/2	=	_____	1/12	=	_____

Convert the decimals into fractions.

0.4	=	_____	0.3	=	_____
0.9	=	_____	0.8	=	_____
0.2	=	_____	0.1	=	_____
0.11	=	_____	0.6	=	_____

Write down the number names for the following decimal fractions:

2/10	=	two-tenths		
8/10	=	_____		
2/9	=	_____		
3/10	=	_____		
7/8	=	_____		
2/7	=	_____		
3/4	=	_____		

3/7	=	three-sevenths
4/7	=	_____
3/5	=	_____
9/10	=	_____
5/6	=	_____
1/7	=	_____
4/5	=	_____

Write down the fractions for the following number names:

Three-tenths	=	3/10
Two-fifths	=	_____
One-ninth	=	_____
Six-eighths	=	_____
Two-ninths	=	_____
Six-sevenths	=	_____

Two-fifths	=	2/5
Nine-tenths	=	_____
Three-fifths	=	_____
One-tenths	=	_____
Seven-ninths	=	_____
Two-sevenths	=	_____

Complete the following:

Three-fifths = Six-tenths = 0.6

0.5 = _____ - tenths = _____ - halves

0.4 = _____ - fifths = _____ - tenths

____ = five - fifths = _____ - tenths

____ - fifths = eight - tenths = 0.____

Complete the following:

_3_ squares = 3/10

= 0._____

= _____-tenths

____ squares = ____/10

= 0._____

= _____-tenths

____ squares = ____/10

= 0._____

= _____-tenths

____ squares = ____/10

= 0._____

= _____-tenths

Complete the table.

Parts in 10	Tenths	Fraction	Decimal
6	Six-tenths	6/10	0.6
1			
9			
2			
8			

Exercise 38

Relationship Between Units of Measurement		
1 kg = 1000 g 1 g = 0.001 kg	1 l = 1000 ml	1 ml = 0.001 l
1 km = 1000 m 1 m = 0.001 km		
1 m = 100 cm 1 cm = 0.01 m		

Convert the following into grams or kilograms:

400 g = _____ kg   1200 g = _____ kg

_____ g = 7.1 kg   _____ g = 3 kg

Convert the following into metres or kilometres:

9500 m = _____ km   2000 m = _____ km

_____ m = 4.5 km   _____ m = 10 km

Convert the following into litres or millilitres:

5200 ml = _____ l   3700 ml = _____ l

_____ ml = 2.2 l   _____ ml = 8 l

Convert the following into metres or centimetres:

340 cm = _____ m   890 cm = _____ m

_____ cm = 1.5 m   _____ cm = 6.2 m

Add the following:

	m	cm
	2	42
+	1	76
	4	18

4m ____ 18cm ____

	l	ml
	6	10
+	3	90

____

	kg	g
	4	25
+	3	74

____

	l	ml
	6	12
+	3	11

____

	km	m
	9	24
+		23

____

	l	ml
	2	33
+	3	22

____

	kg	g
	8	40
+	1	45

____

	m	cm
	4	63
+	5	12

____

	km	m
	2	54
+	7	18

____

Subtract the following:

	l	ml
	3	56
−	2	21
	1	35

1l   35ml

	km	m
	9	12
−	7	10

_____

	kg	g
	6	94
−	4	76

_____

	m	cm
	7	28
−	1	20

_____

	kg	g
	5	89
−	2	84

_____

	km	m
	2	47
−	1	32

_____

	m	cm
	4	99
−	4	11

_____

	l	ml
	3	50
−	2	25

_____

	km	m
	6	95
−	5	90

_____

Write each of the following in metres only.

200 cm = _____

2.4 km = _____

46 cm = _____

1.84 km = _____

145 cm = _____

12 km = _____

9.5 km = _____

65 cm = _____

Write each of the following in kilograms only.

565 g = _____

4600 g = _____

400 g = _____

1230 g = _____

250 g = _____

770 g = _____

85 g = _____

320 g = _____

Write each of the following in litres only.

4500 ml = _____

460 ml = _____

2100 ml = _____

240 ml = _____

980 ml = _____

120 ml = _____

1245 ml = _____

368 ml = _____

Write each of the following in kilometres only.

20000 cm   =   1200 m   =

340 m   =   450000 cm =

460 m   =   7685 m   =

Write each of the following in millilitres only.

4.2 l =   8.9 l =

3.1 l =   7.5 l =

6 l   =   12.2 l =

Write each of the following in centimetres only.

0.05 km =   0.86 km =

4.2 m =   1.2 m =

7.3 m =   6.7 m =

Write each of the following in grams only.

3 kg   =   5.5 kg   =

2.4 kg =   13.4 kg   =

8.1 kg =   10 kg   =

Multiply the following:

20 kg x 5 = <u>100</u> kg   33 l x 3   = ____ l   25 l x 4   = ____ l

12 kg x 3 = ____ kg   12 kg x 3 = ____ kg   5 kg x 4 = ____ kg

14 l x 5   = ____ l   46 kg x 2 = ____ kg   24 m x 3 = ____ m

6 l x 12   = ____ l   11 kg x 7   = ____ kg   13 m x 6   = ____ m

2 km x 6   = ____ km   30 km x 5 = ____ m   11 km x 4 = ____ m

8 km x 8   = ____ km   18 km x 2 = ____ m   44 m x 2 = ____ m

2 km x 6   = ____ km   3 m x 7   = ____ m   10 l x 8   = ____ l

30 km x 3 = ____ km   9 m x 8   = ____ m   15 m x 5 = ____ m

Divide the following:

25 m ÷ 5 = __5__ m   56 m ÷ 7 = ____ m   24 m ÷ 4 = ____ m

42 m ÷ 6 = ____ m   21 m ÷ 3 = ____ m   45 m ÷ 9 = ____ m

46 ml ÷ 2 = ____ ml   20 ml ÷ 5 = ____ ml   81 ml ÷ 9 = ____ ml

10 ml ÷ 1 = ____ ml   77 ml ÷ 11 = ____ ml   32 ml ÷ 4 = ____ ml

49 g ÷ 7 = ____ g   40 g ÷ 4 = ____ g   24 g ÷ 3 = ____ g

72 g ÷ 9 = ____ g   36 g ÷ 6 = ____ g   46 g ÷ 2 = ____ g

45 cm ÷ 9 = ____ cm   90 cm ÷ 10 = ____ cm   30 cm ÷ 6 = ____ cm

22 cm ÷ 2 = ____ cm   65 cm ÷ 5 = ____ cm   27 cm ÷ 3 = ____ cm

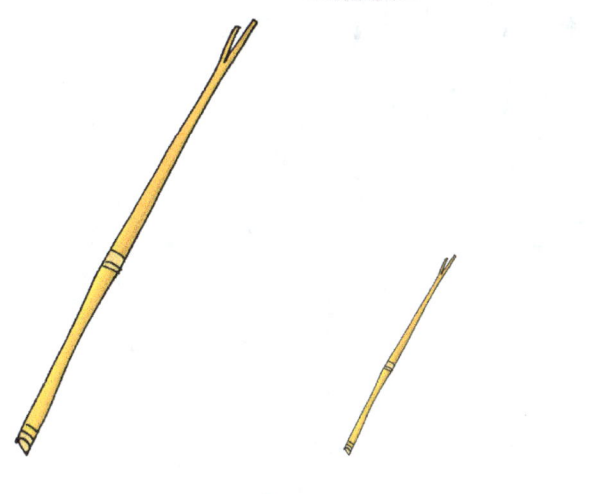
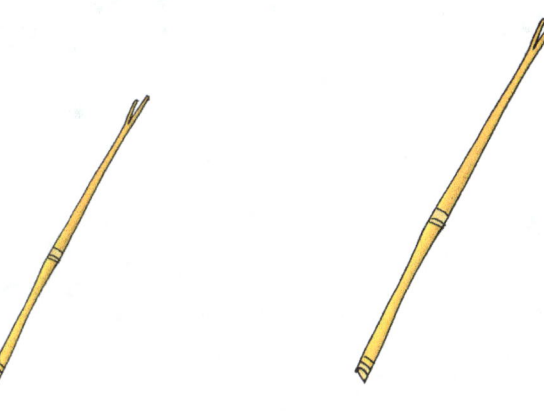

A – 8.2 cm   B – 2.9 cm   C – 5.5 cm   D – 7.6 cm

Solve the following:

Length of A + length of B   = _____ cm = _____ m

Length of C + length of D   = _____ cm = _____ m

Length of A + length of C   = _____ cm = _____ m

Length of B + length of D   = _____ cm = _____ m

Length of A + length of D   = _____ cm = _____ m

Length of B + length of C   = _____ cm = _____ m

Length of A + length of B

+ length of C + length D   = _____ cm = _____ m

2 (length of A + length of D)

– 2 (length B + length C)   = _____ cm = _____ m

Exercise 46

Add the following and complete the table below:

A	B	C	D	Total
550 cm	230 cm	300 cm	400 cm	1480 cm
2 kg	900 g	3 kg	100 g	
420 km	680 km	1500 km	500 km	
110 kg	340 kg	120 kg	640 kg	
1900 ml	1200 ml	15 l	15 l	
2 kg	7 kg	9 kg	3 kg	
146 g	141 g	211 g	5 kg	
234 l	829 l	990 l	125 l	
620 cm	4 m	9 m	220 cm	
2500 g	2 kg	5.5 kg	4700 g	
780 km	180 km	550 km	230 km	
278 l	920 l	430 l	510 l	
750 cm	3 m	5 m	950 cm	
8.1 kg	2100 g	9.2 kg	3.5 kg	
890 cm	200 cm	560 cm	920 cm	

Study the pictures below and tell whether the line on each of them is the line of symmetry. Write Yes or No.

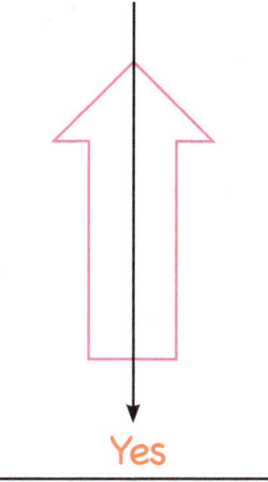

Yes
_____

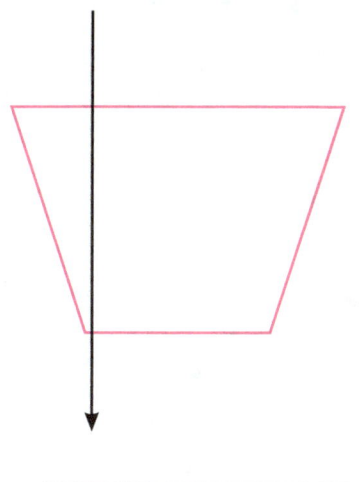

_____

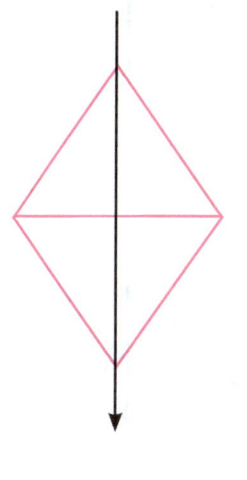

_____

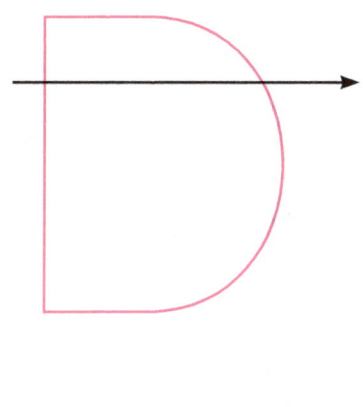

_____

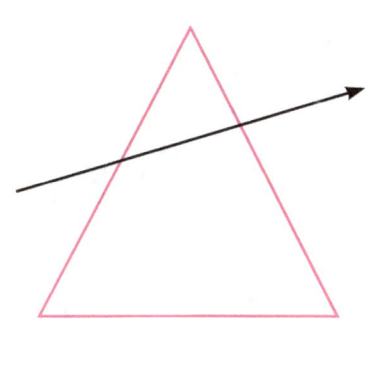

_____

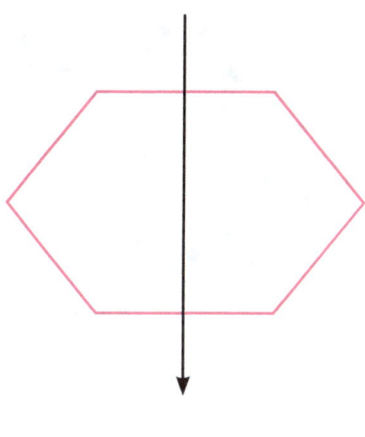

_____

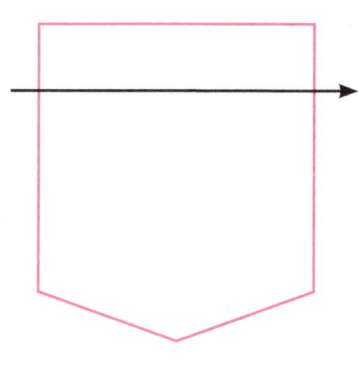

_____

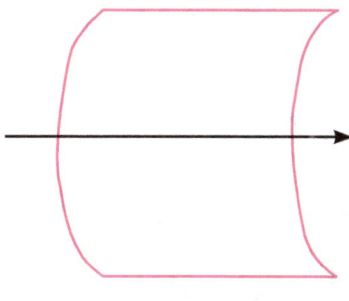

_____

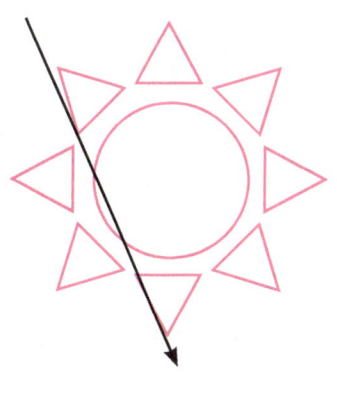

_____

Draw the line of symmetry for the following shapes:

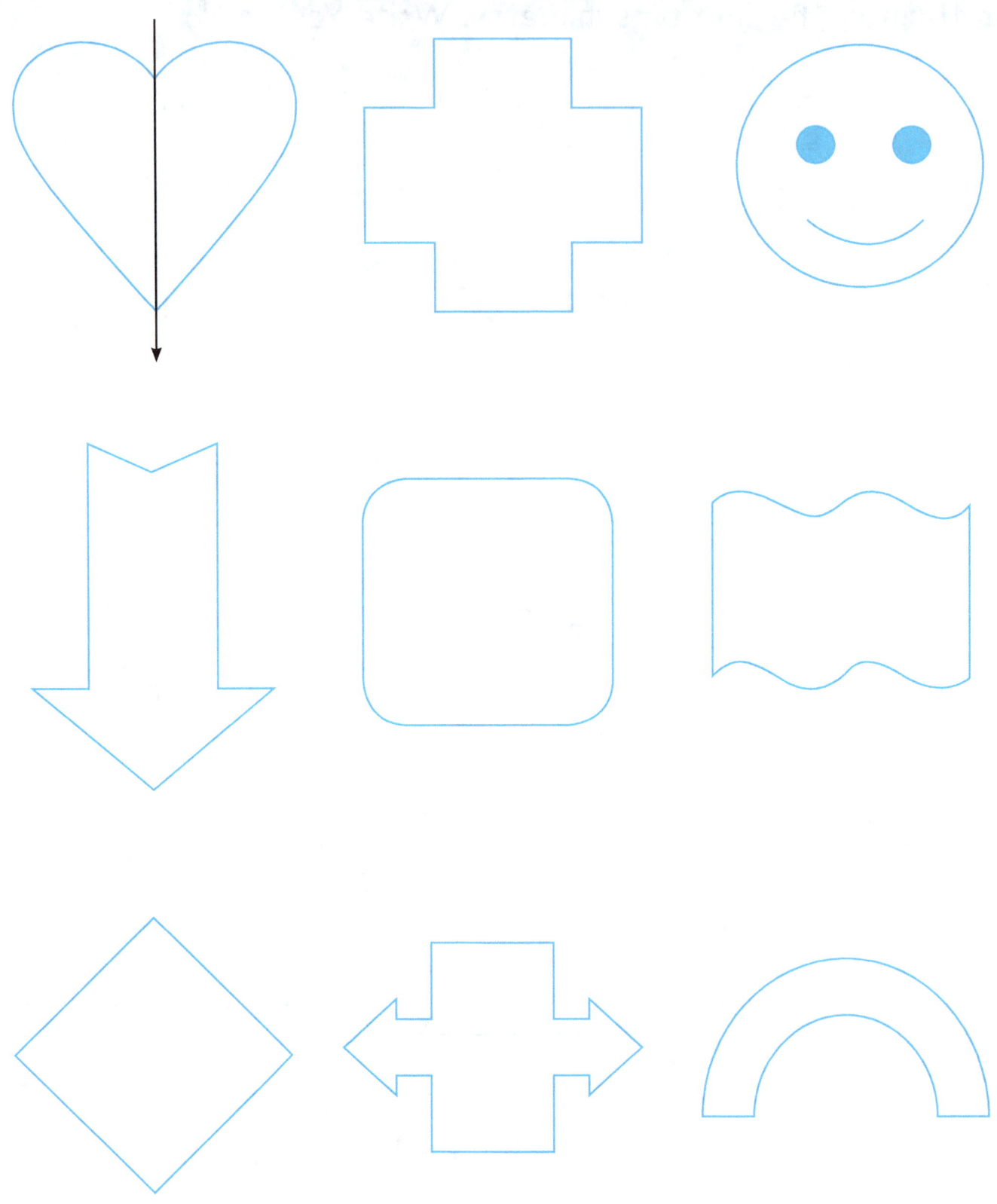

One line of symmetry has been drawn on each shape. Now draw a different line of symmetry for each.

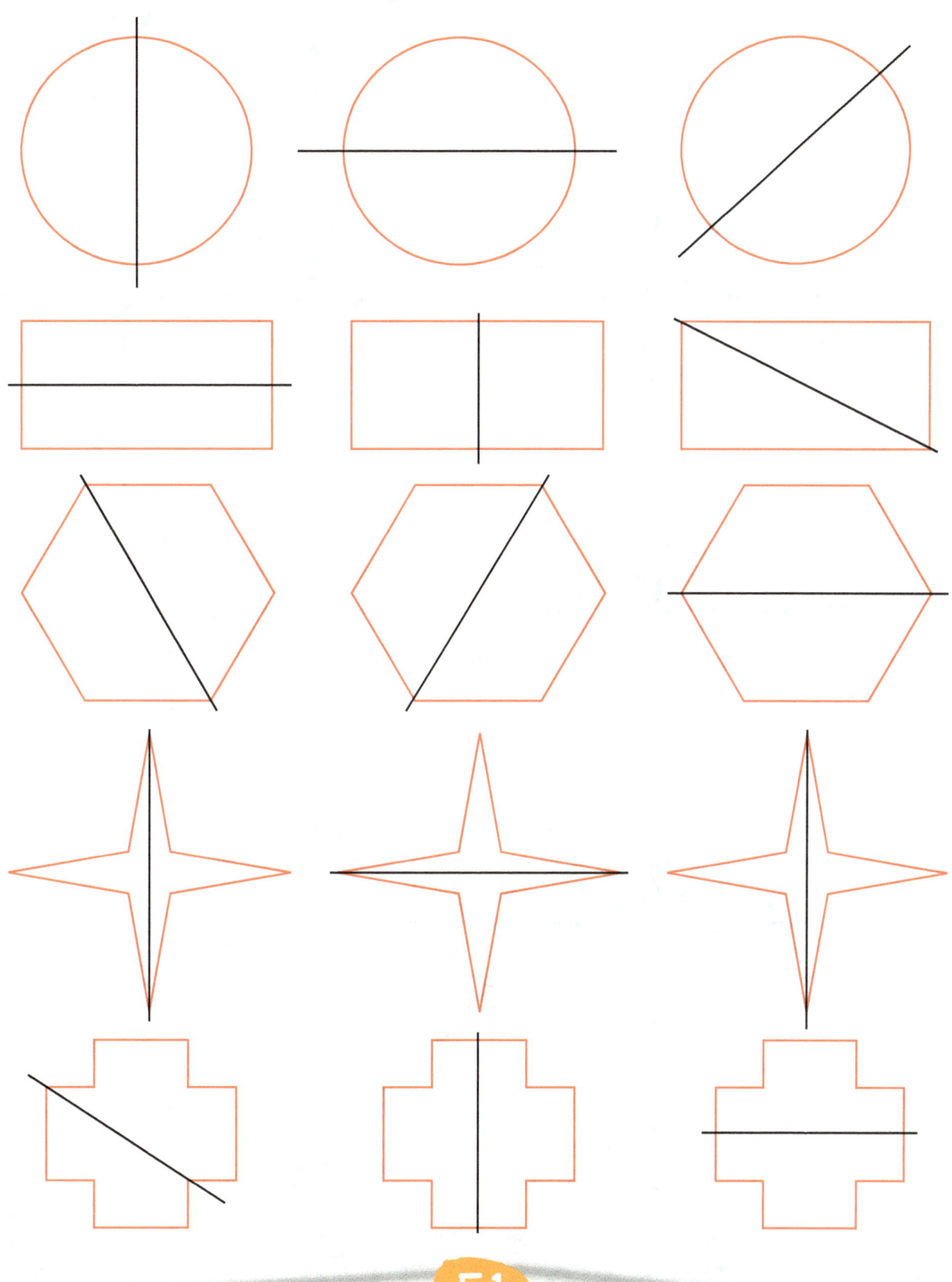

Complete the following factor trees:

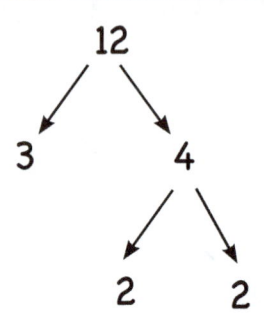

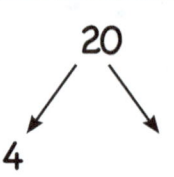

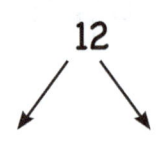

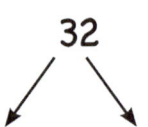

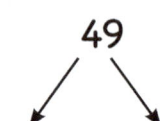

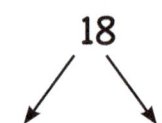

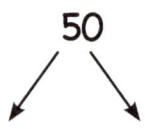

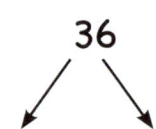

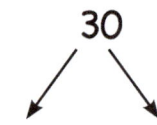

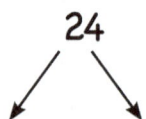

Exercise 51

Find the least common multiple (L.C.M.) of each of the following pairs:

Numbers	L.C.M	Numbers	L.C.M
10, 60	60	5, 10	
6, 20		50, 80	
15, 45		4, 60	
8, 24		2, 36	
20, 40		32, 48	
3, 12		24, 27	
5, 6		11, 12	
18, 30		3, 51	

Find the highest common factor (H.C.F.) of each of the following pairs:

Numbers	H.C.F	Numbers	H.C.F
8, 16	8	18, 12	
21, 18		15, 40	
15, 45		15, 6	
21, 18		15, 25	
21, 6		20, 18	
30, 35		21, 27	
4, 12		20, 30	
8, 24		15, 13	

Complete the following sets of numbers:

X = {factors of 14} = {1, 2, 7, 14}

Z = {factors of 23} = {_____}

A = {factors of 70} = {_____}

N = {factors of 10} = {_____}

S = {factors of 15} = {_____}

J = {factors of 6} = {_____}

R = {factors of 20} = {_____}

T = {factors of 60} = {_____}

Q = {factors of 9} = {_____}

O = {factors of 63} = {_____}

P = {factors of 56} = {_____}

M = {factors of 90} = {_____}

L = {factors of 33} = {_____}

N = {factors of 42} = {_____}

D = {factors of 19} = {_____}

C = {factors of 8} = {_____}

Y = {factors of 21} = {_____}

U = {factors of 11} = {_____}

Encircle the prime numbers in the number grid given below:

(1)	2	3	4	5	6	7	8	9	10
11	12	13	14	15	16	17	18	19	20
21	22	23	24	25	26	27	28	29	30
31	32	33	34	35	36	37	38	39	40
41	42	43	44	45	46	47	48	49	50
51	52	53	54	55	56	57	58	59	60
61	62	63	64	65	66	67	68	69	70
71	72	73	74	75	76	77	78	79	80
81	82	83	84	85	86	87	88	89	90
91	92	93	94	95	96	97	98	99	100

Write all the prime numbers between:

20 and 30   _____23, 29_____

10 and 25   _____

55 and 80   _____

35 and 50   _____

45 and 90   _____

85 and 100   _____

Exercise 54

Solve:

Find the smallest number that 4 and 5 can divide without a remainder.

20

What is the least number that is exactly divisible by 12, 15 and 20?

Divide the L.C.M. of 16 and 24 by that of 3 and 6.

Divide the L.C.M. of 20 and 25 by the L.C.M. of 4 and 5.

Find the L.C.M. of 10, 12 and 15.

Solve:

Find the sum of the H.C.F. of 4 and 8 and the H.C.F. of 6 and 12.

10

Multiply the H.C.F. of 6 and 8 and the H.C.F. of 15 and 25.

Find the difference between the H.C.F. of 14 and 21 and the H.C.F. of 30 and 45.

Divide the H.C.F. of 66 and 90 by 3.

Find the H.C.F. of 21, 63 and 105.

Look at the pattern carefully and fill in the empty boxes with the correct number. The first one has been done for you.

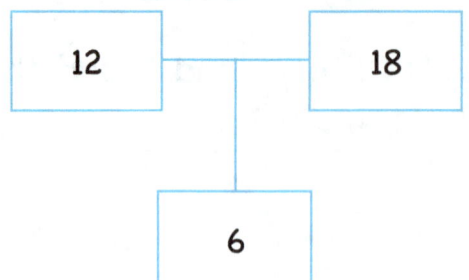

1.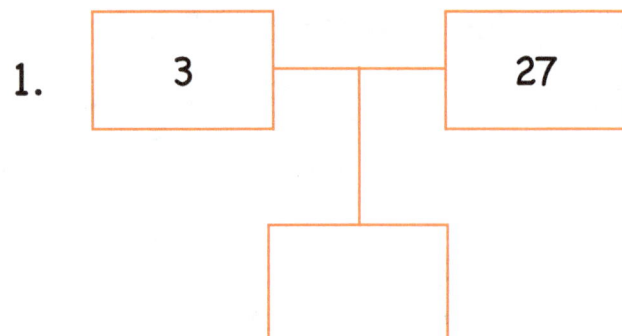

2.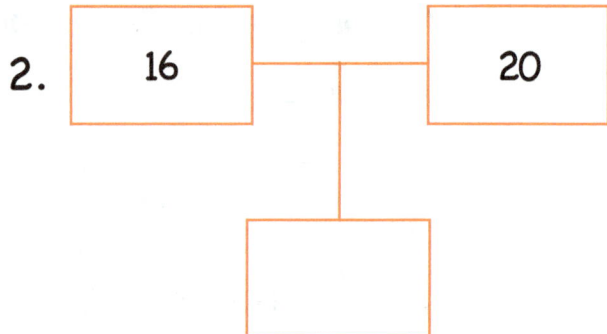

3.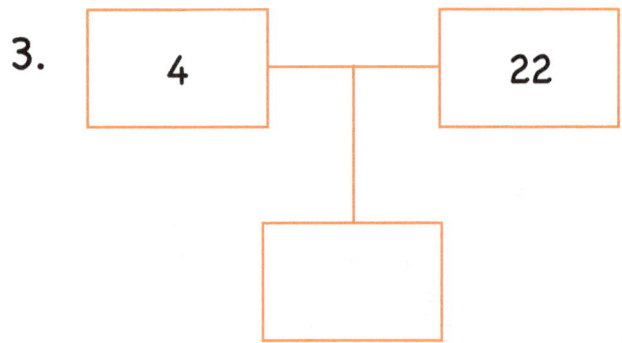

4.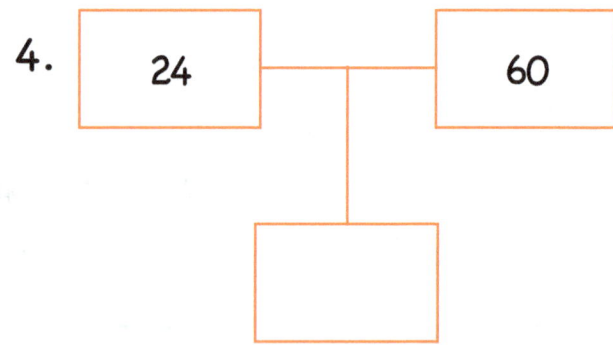

5.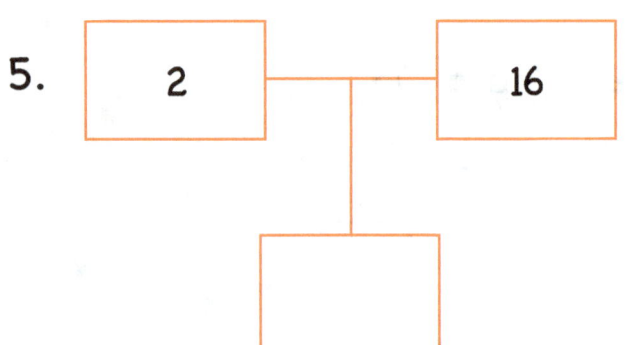

6.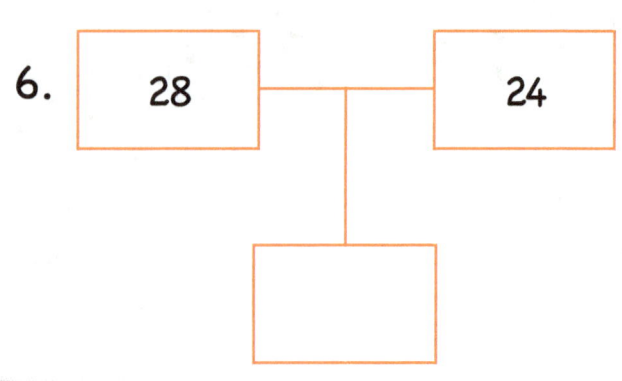

Mark the multiples of $\frac{1}{2}$ on the number line below.

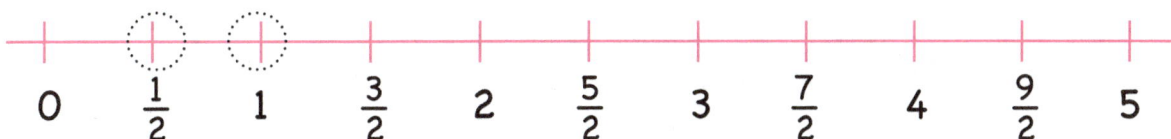

Mark the multiples of $\frac{1}{6}$ on the number line below.

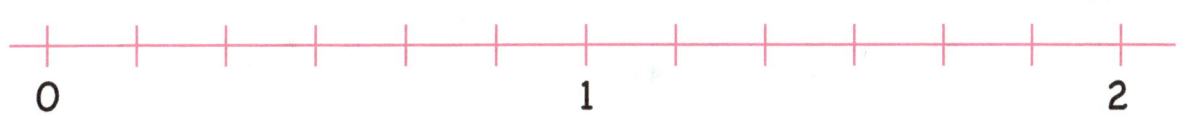

Mark the multiples of $\frac{1}{4}$ on the number line below.

Mark the multiples of $\frac{1}{8}$ on the number line below.

Mark the multiples of $\frac{1}{3}$ on the number line below.

Exercise 58

Write any three equal fractions for the following fractions:

$\frac{1}{2}$	$\frac{2}{4}$	$\frac{3}{6}$	$\frac{4}{8}$
$\frac{2}{7}$			
$\frac{3}{4}$			
$\frac{2}{5}$			
$\frac{1}{8}$			
$\frac{3}{7}$			
$\frac{1}{10}$			
$\frac{5}{9}$			
$\frac{1}{9}$			
$\frac{2}{10}$			
$\frac{6}{7}$			
$\frac{3}{5}$			
$\frac{1}{4}$			
$\frac{6}{8}$			
$\frac{5}{5}$			

Exercise 59

Fill in the blanks.

1. $\dfrac{1}{10} = \dfrac{3}{\boxed{30}}$

6. $\dfrac{8}{10} = \dfrac{\square}{20}$

2. $\dfrac{1}{3} = \dfrac{\square}{9}$

7. $\dfrac{1}{\square} = \dfrac{12}{24}$

3. $\dfrac{3}{5} = \dfrac{15}{\square}$

8. $\dfrac{8}{9} = \dfrac{40}{\square}$

4. $\dfrac{\square}{8} = \dfrac{25}{40}$

9. $\dfrac{3}{4} = \dfrac{\square}{24}$

5. $\dfrac{2}{7} = \dfrac{\square}{35}$

10. $\dfrac{2}{7} = \dfrac{\square}{28}$

Are the following pairs of fractions equal fractions? Write Yes or No.

1. $\dfrac{2}{8}, \dfrac{1}{4}$ ___Yes___

6. $\dfrac{3}{4}, \dfrac{12}{16}$ _____

2. $\dfrac{5}{5}, \dfrac{2}{10}$ _____

7. $\dfrac{3}{4}, \dfrac{9}{12}$ _____

3. $\dfrac{1}{5}, \dfrac{5}{15}$ _____

8. $\dfrac{2}{3}, \dfrac{12}{18}$ _____

4. $\dfrac{2}{3}, \dfrac{6}{9}$ _____

9. $\dfrac{1}{2}, \dfrac{13}{26}$ _____

5. $\dfrac{6}{12}, \dfrac{1}{2}$ _____

10. $\dfrac{6}{7}, \dfrac{12}{14}$ _____

Put the correct symbol <, > or =.

1. $\frac{2}{3} > \frac{1}{6}$

2. $\frac{1}{2} \underline{\hspace{1cm}} \frac{4}{10}$

3. $\frac{3}{4} \underline{\hspace{1cm}} \frac{6}{12}$

4. $\frac{1}{12} \underline{\hspace{1cm}} \frac{5}{6}$

5. $\frac{1}{7} \underline{\hspace{1cm}} \frac{3}{7}$

6. $\frac{8}{9} \underline{\hspace{1cm}} \frac{6}{9}$

7. $\frac{3}{5} \underline{\hspace{1cm}} \frac{1}{7}$

8. $\frac{2}{5} \underline{\hspace{1cm}} \frac{7}{10}$

9. $\frac{1}{8} \underline{\hspace{1cm}} \frac{3}{5}$

10. $\frac{7}{8} \underline{\hspace{1cm}} \frac{3}{4}$

Arrange the fractions in ascending order.

1. $\frac{1}{3}, \frac{1}{2}, \frac{1}{6}$ $\underline{\quad \frac{1}{6}, \frac{1}{3}, \frac{1}{2} \quad}$

2. $\frac{4}{5}, \frac{1}{15}, \frac{4}{10}$ $\underline{\hspace{3cm}}$

3. $\frac{1}{4}, \frac{1}{10}, \frac{1}{7}$ $\underline{\hspace{3cm}}$

4. $\frac{7}{8}, \frac{3}{4}, \frac{4}{5}$ $\underline{\hspace{3cm}}$

5. $\frac{1}{2}, \frac{7}{8}, \frac{3}{4}$ $\underline{\hspace{3cm}}$

Arrange the fractions in descending order.

1. $\frac{2}{3}, \frac{5}{6}, \frac{2}{6}$ $\underline{\quad \frac{5}{6}, \frac{2}{3}, \frac{2}{6} \quad}$

2. $\frac{1}{5}, \frac{4}{5}, \frac{2}{5}$ $\underline{\hspace{3cm}}$

3. $\frac{7}{9}, \frac{2}{3}, \frac{5}{6}$ $\underline{\hspace{3cm}}$

4. $\frac{1}{5}, \frac{1}{5}, \frac{1}{3}$ $\underline{\hspace{3cm}}$

5. $\frac{2}{3}, \frac{5}{6}, \frac{1}{12}$ $\underline{\hspace{3cm}}$

Convert the following mixed fractions into improper fractions and decimals.

$8 \left(\frac{2}{3} \right)$ $\frac{26}{3}$ 8.66

$3 \left(\frac{3}{4} \right)$

$1 \left(\frac{1}{5} \right)$

$5 \left(\frac{2}{3} \right)$

$3 \left(\frac{4}{5} \right)$

$5 \left(\frac{1}{2} \right)$

$7 \left(\frac{4}{5} \right)$

$4 \left(\frac{9}{10} \right)$

$2 \left(\frac{2}{3} \right)$

Convert the following improper fractions into mixed fractions.

$\frac{9}{4}$ $2 \left(\frac{1}{4} \right)$ $\frac{17}{3}$

$\frac{33}{4}$ $\frac{21}{8}$

$\frac{11}{4}$ $\frac{47}{5}$

$\frac{10}{3}$

$\frac{13}{2}$

Add the following fractions:

$5\left(\dfrac{1}{3}\right)$ + $1\left(\dfrac{3}{4}\right)$ = _____ $7\left(\dfrac{1}{12}\right)$_____

$2\left(\dfrac{5}{6}\right)$ + $2\left(\dfrac{3}{4}\right)$ = _____

$5\left(\dfrac{2}{3}\right)$ + $6\left(\dfrac{5}{8}\right)$ = _____

$8\left(\dfrac{1}{2}\right)$ + $1\left(\dfrac{2}{3}\right)$ = _____

$1\left(\dfrac{7}{8}\right)$ + $3\left(\dfrac{1}{2}\right)$ = _____

$8\left(\dfrac{1}{4}\right)$ + $2\left(\dfrac{7}{8}\right)$ = _____

$2\left(\dfrac{3}{4}\right)$ + $9\left(\dfrac{1}{2}\right)$ = _____

Subtract the following fractions:

$4\left(\dfrac{1}{4}\right)$ − $1\left(\dfrac{3}{4}\right)$ = _____ $2\left(\dfrac{1}{2}\right)$_____

$2\left(\dfrac{1}{4}\right)$ − $1\left(\dfrac{1}{2}\right)$ = _____

$5\left(\dfrac{1}{6}\right)$ − $3\left(\dfrac{1}{3}\right)$ = _____

$3\left(\dfrac{1}{2}\right)$ − $1\left(\dfrac{3}{4}\right)$ = _____

$7\left(\dfrac{1}{3}\right)$ − $3\left(\dfrac{5}{6}\right)$ = _____

$8\left(\dfrac{1}{3}\right)$ − $1\left(\dfrac{5}{9}\right)$ = _____

$2\left(\dfrac{1}{5}\right)$ − $1\left(\dfrac{1}{4}\right)$ = _____

Arrange each group of decimal fraction in ascending order:

0.2, 0.5, 0.75, 0.25 _____ 0.2, 0.25, 0.5, 0.75 _____

0.3, 0.4, 0.25 _____

0.7, 0.75, 0.25 _____

0.54, 0.8, 0.45 _____

0.03, 0.3, 0.5 _____

0.32, 0.48, 0.24 _____

0.93, 0.84, 0.72 _____

0.2, 0.12, 0.21 _____

Arrange each group of decimal fraction in descending order:

0.23, 0.46, 0.75 _____ 0.75, 0.46, 0.23 _____

0.37, 0.25, 0.2 _____

0.02, 0.03, 0.04 _____

0.67, 0.89, 0.12 _____

0.68, 0.35, 0.67 _____

0.15, 0.17, 0.11 _____

0.9, 0.2, 0.6 _____

Add the following decimals:

37.04 + 25.6   =   <u>   62.64   </u>

42.44 + 15.17   =   <u>   </u>

32.13 + 78.15   =   <u>   </u>

15.54 + 46.63   =   <u>   </u>

14.05 + 19.18   =   <u>   </u>

23.02 + 21.07   =   <u>   </u>

75.25 + 25.75   =   <u>   </u>

51.42 + 28.8   =   <u>   </u>

Subtract the following decimals:

91.56 – 87.32   =   <u>   4.24   </u>

33.8 – 28.9   =   <u>   </u>

45.05 – 22.03   =   <u>   </u>

64.65 – 18.16   =   <u>   </u>

46.1 – 37.32   =   <u>   </u>

25.46 – 20.6   =   <u>   </u>

40.5 – 11.5   =   <u>   </u>

68.15 – 13.13   =   <u>   </u>

Multiply the following:

25.05 x 2   =   _____50.1_____

15.1 x 5   =   _____

11.25 x 3   =   _____

12.9 x 5   =   _____

42.8 x 4   =   _____

13.3 x 3   =   _____

18.6 x 2   =   _____

10.10 x 6   =   _____

Divide the following:

21.75 ÷ 3   =   _____7.25_____

24.16 ÷ 4   =   _____

28.4 ÷ 2   =   _____

1.23 ÷ 3   =   _____

65.25 ÷ 5   =   _____

49.7 ÷ 7   =   _____

88.11 ÷ 11   =   _____

4.23 ÷ 10   =   _____

Express the following percentages as fractions:

10%	1/10	2%	_____
45%	_____	33%	_____
128%	_____	66%	_____
200%	_____	50%	_____
12%	_____	90%	_____

Express the following fractions as percentages:

$\frac{3}{4}$	75%	$\frac{5}{5}$	_____
$\frac{7}{10}$	_____	$\frac{2}{4}$	_____
$\frac{3}{10}$	_____	$\frac{1}{4}$	_____
$\frac{2}{5}$	_____	$\frac{2}{25}$	_____
$\frac{1}{20}$	_____	$\frac{3}{5}$	_____

Express the following percentages as decimals:

16%	0.16	22%	_____
50%	_____	68%	_____
110%	_____	96%	_____
500%	_____	42%	_____
20%	_____	75%	_____

Exercise 67

Put the correct symbol (>, <, =) in the blanks.

25% __>__ $\frac{1}{5}$

7/9 ____ 90%

$\frac{3}{4}$ ____ 0.5

0.6 ____ 6%

$\frac{1}{10}$ ____ 20%

0.5 ____ $\frac{2}{3}$

$\frac{1}{8}$ ____ 40%

0.2 ____ $\frac{1}{2}$

30% ____ $\frac{6}{20}$

31% ____ 0.22

Write in ascending order.

$\frac{7}{8}$, 0.7, 10% $\underline{\quad 10\%, 0.7, \frac{7}{8} \quad}$

80%, $\frac{2}{3}$, 0.12   _____

31%, $\frac{1}{3}$, 0.12   _____

$\frac{3}{5}$, 0.5, 20%   _____

0.75, 30%, $\frac{1}{4}$ _____

Write in descending order.

$\frac{3}{4}$, 80%, 0.25 $\underline{\quad 80\%, \frac{3}{4}, 0.25 \quad}$

$\frac{3}{4}$, 2%, 0.5   _____

$\frac{4}{5}$, 60%, 0.5   _____

0.76, 25%, $\frac{11}{10}$ _____

0.75, $\frac{3}{4}$, 77%   _____

69

Express the following ratios in the simplest form.

4:12	_1:3_	18:24	_____
3:1.5	_____	25:10	_____
18:6	_____	16:48	_____
24:36	_____	13:39	_____
25:150	_____	24:36	_____

Find the value of y in the following:

$1 : 5 = 10 : y$

_____ $y = 50$ _____

$y : 9 = 15 : 45$

_____

$11 : 2 = 88 : y$

_____

$8 : 2 = y : 12$

_____

$y : 5 = 3 : 15$

_____

$4 : 1 = 28 : y$

_____

$5 : 6 = 10 : y$

_____

$2 : y = 8 : 40$

_____

$y : 3 = 12 : 36$

_____

$125 : y = 1 : 250$

_____

$4 : 5 = 16 : y$

_____

$y : 35 = 1 : 5$

_____

$y : 12 = 25 : 5$

_____

$3 : 4 = y : 32$

_____

Solve

The ratio of boys to girls in a certain class is 11:13. If there are 72 pupils in the class, how many of them are girls?

13/24 x 72 = 39

Divide 108 pencils between Tom and Jack in the ratio of 4:5.

Kim and Den share 78 mangoes in the ratio of 3:8 respectively. How many mangoes does Kim get?

12-years old Albert and his 8-year old brother Brown share a 30 cm long sugarcane in the ratio of their ages. Find the length of the sugarcane received by Brown.

Divide 368 bags of cement between two men in the ratio of 5:3.

Exercise 70

Classify and measure the angles given below:

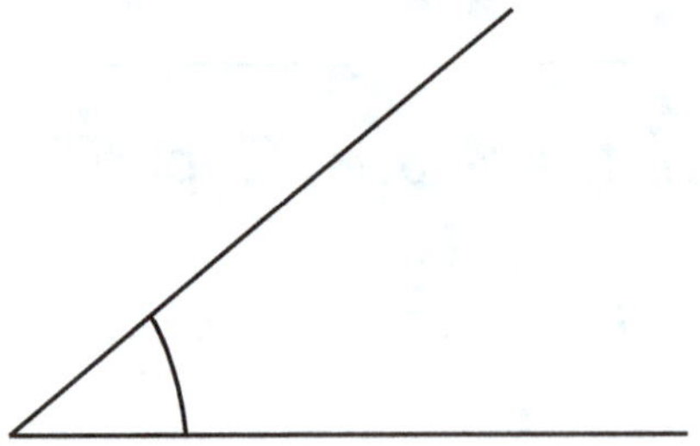

Acute angle

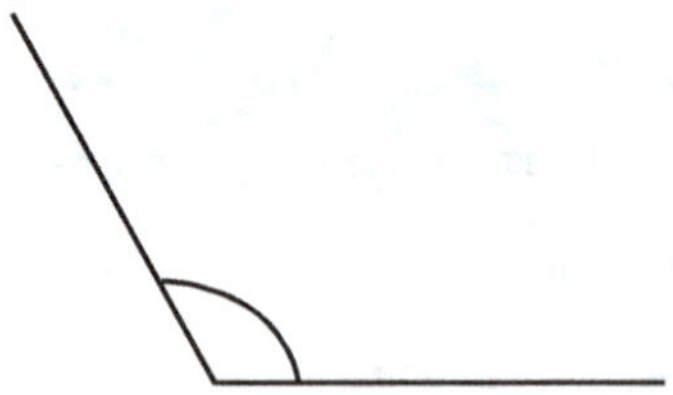

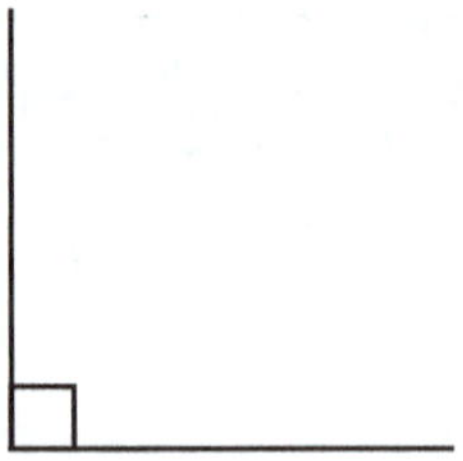

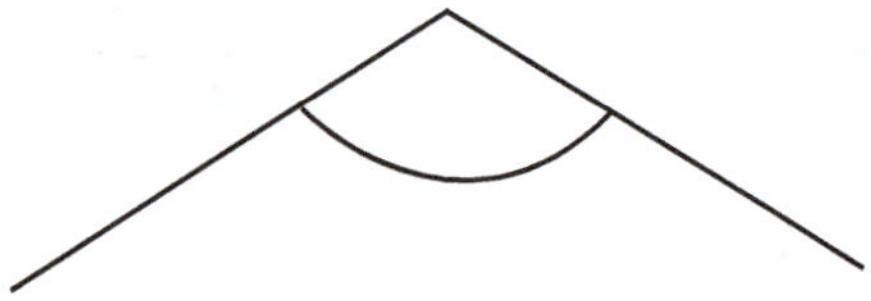

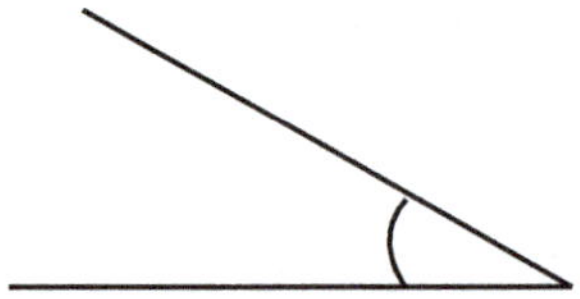

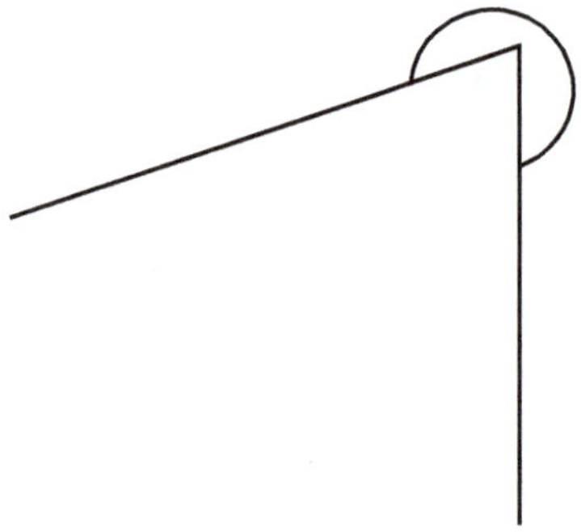

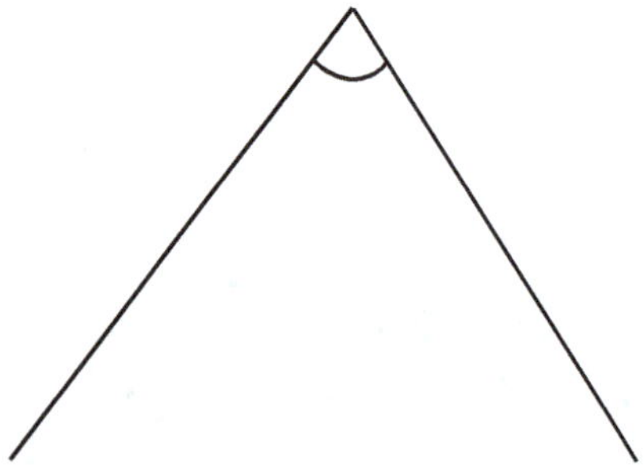

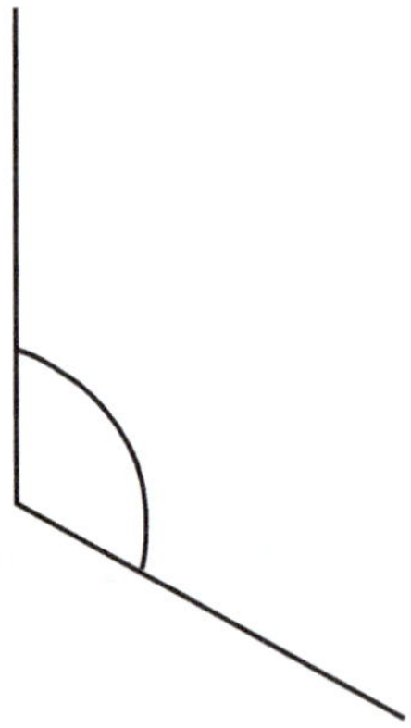

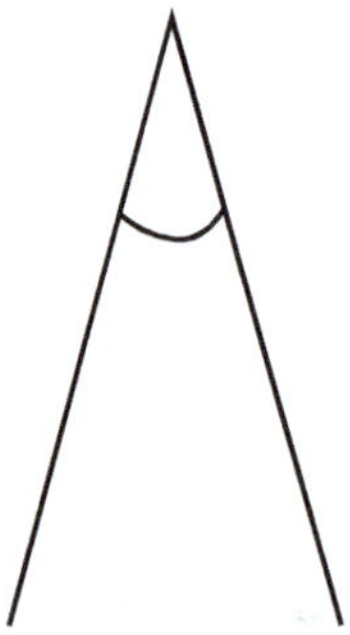

----------- ----------- -----------

----------- ----------- -----------

----------- ----------- -----------

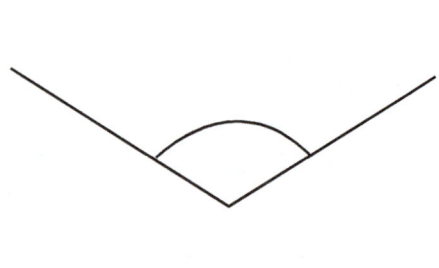

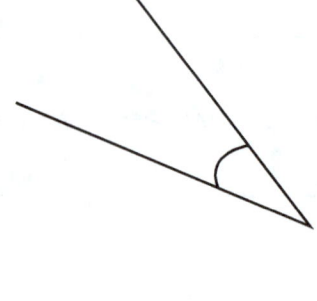

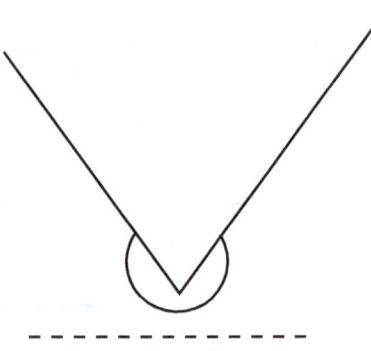

----------- Exercise ----------- -----------

Find the area and perimeter of the following squares:

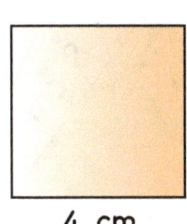

4 cm

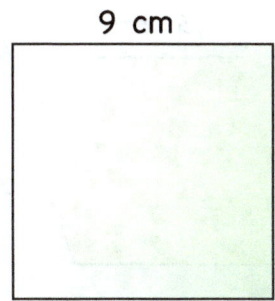

9 cm

5.5 cm

Area ___16 cm²___

Perimeter ___16 cm___

Area _____

Perimeter _____

Area _____

Perimeter _____

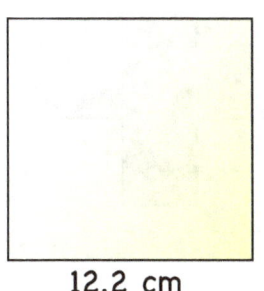

12.2 cm

1.9 cm

10.10 cm

Area _____

Perimeter _____

Area _____

Perimeter _____

Area _____

Perimeter _____

Find the area and perimeter of the following rectangles:

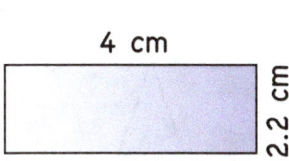

4 cm

2.2 cm

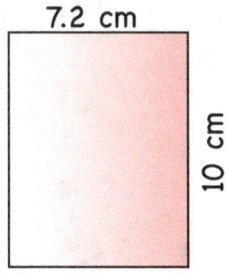

7.2 cm

10 cm

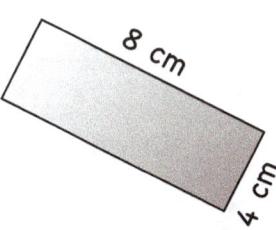

8 cm

4 cm

Area ___8.8 cm²___

Perimeter ___12.4 cm___

Area _____

Perimeter _____

Area _____

Perimeter _____

Find the perimeter of the following shapes:

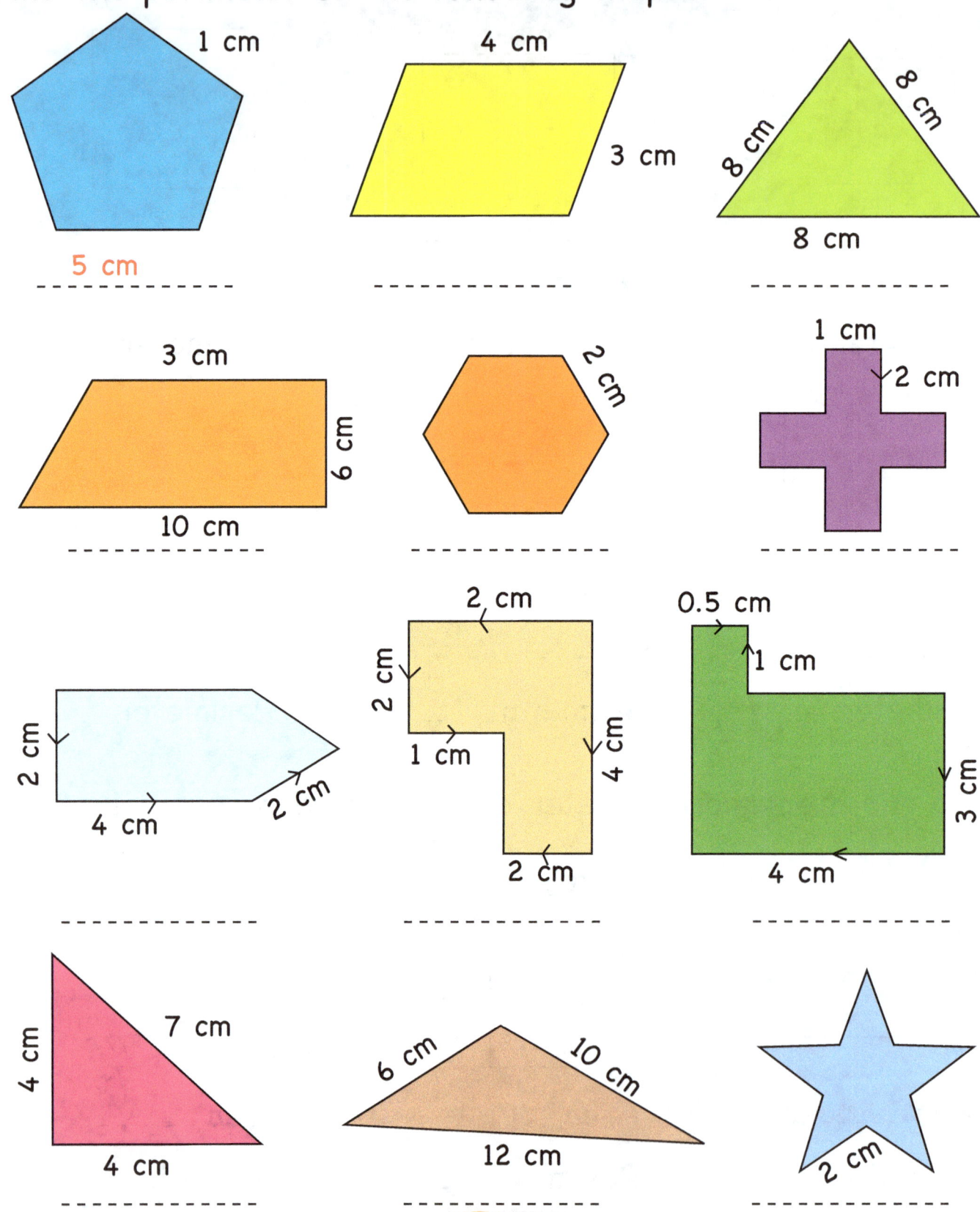

1 cm

5 cm

- - - - - - - - - - - -

4 cm

3 cm

- - - - - - - - - - - -

8 cm

8 cm

8 cm

- - - - - - - - - - - -

3 cm

6 cm

10 cm

- - - - - - - - - - - -

2 cm

- - - - - - - - - - - -

1 cm

2 cm

- - - - - - - - - - - -

2 cm

4 cm

2 cm

- - - - - - - - - - - -

2 cm

2 cm

1 cm

4 cm

2 cm

- - - - - - - - - - - -

0.5 cm

1 cm

3 cm

4 cm

- - - - - - - - - - - -

4 cm

7 cm

4 cm

- - - - - - - - - - - -

6 cm

10 cm

12 cm

- - - - - - - - - - - -

2 cm

- - - - - - - - - - - -

Exercise 73

Find the area and circumference of the following circles:

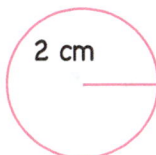

Area <u>4π cm²</u>

Circumference <u>4π cm</u>

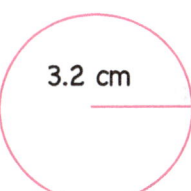

Area _____

Circumference _____

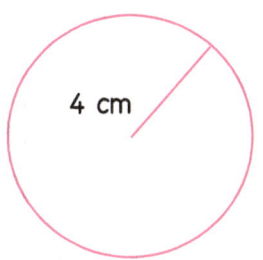

Area _____

Circumference _____

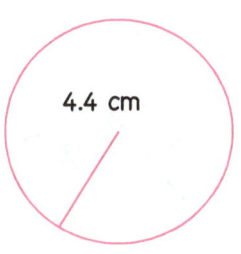

Area _____

Circumference _____

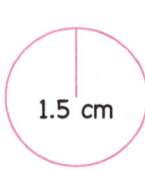

Area _____

Circumference _____

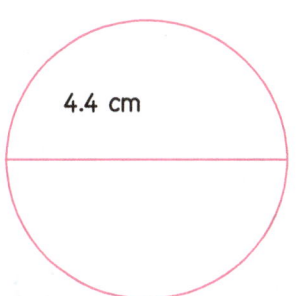

Area _____

Circumference _____

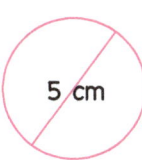

Area _____

Circumference _____

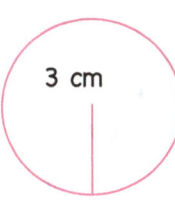

Area _____

Circumference _____

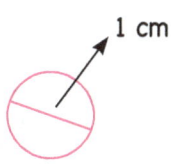

Area _____

Circumference _____

Use the Pythagoras theorem to find the length of the side of the following triangles:

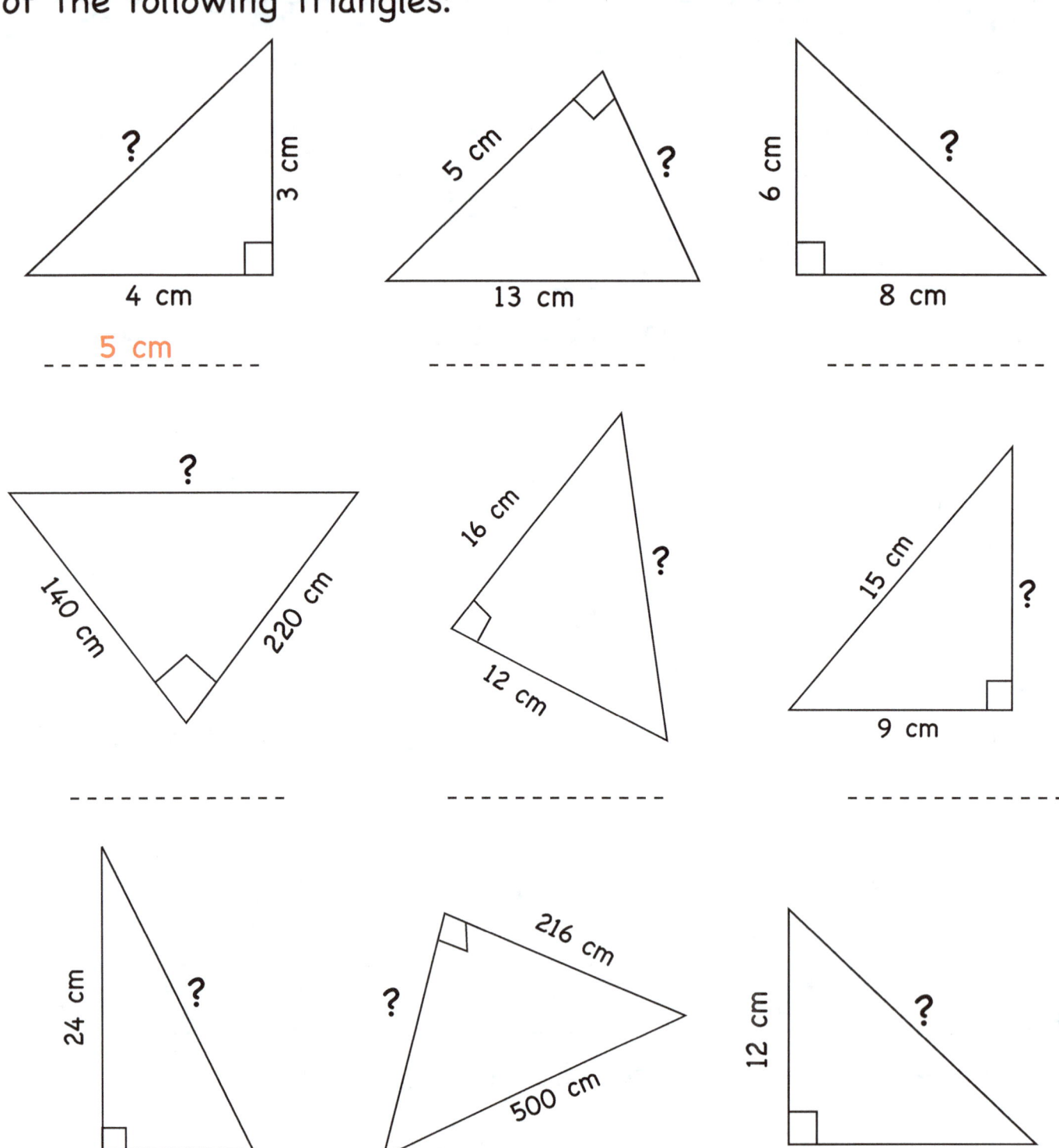

5 cm

- - - - - - - - - - - - - - - - - - - - - - - - - - - - - - - - -

- - - - - - - - - - - - - - - - - - - - - - - - - - - - - - - - -

- - - - - - - - - - - - - - - - - - - - - - - - - - - - - - - - -

Copy and complete:

Rectangle			
Area	Perimeter	Length	Width
22 cm	26 cm	11 cm	2 cm
28 cm	_____	_____	4 cm
_____	18 cm	5 cm	_____
_____	26 cm	_____	7 cm
72 cm	_____	12 cm	_____
56 cm	_____	_____	8 cm

Find the perimeter and length of the squares using the area of the squares given below.

Square		
Area	Perimeter	Length
36 cm²	24 cm	6 cm
6.25 cm²	_____	_____
144 cm²	_____	_____
49 cm²	_____	_____
1.21 cm²	_____	_____
64 cm²	_____	_____

Find the value of x.

$38 + x = 56$ $x = 18$	$x - 64 = 12$ _____	$x - 23 = 35$ _____
$23 + x = 45$ _____	$31 + x = 50$ _____	$61 + x = 99$ _____
$87 - x = 69$ _____	$96 - x = 42$ _____	$72 - x = 18$ _____
$x + 25 = 73$ _____	$x + 14 = 38$ _____	$x - 30 = 39$ _____

Find the value of y.

$2y + 5 = 13$ $y = 4$	$81 - 6y = 9$ _____	$4y - 7 = 18$ _____
$45 - 3y = 0$ _____	$21 + 5y = 36$ _____	$35 + 2y = 55$ _____
$9y - 45 = 45$ _____	$49 - 2y = 33$ _____	$68 - 5y = 8$ _____
$36 + 4y = 40$ _____	$6y + 11 = 35$ _____	$11y - 13 = 64$ _____

Add the following like fractions:

$\frac{1}{2} + \frac{3}{2} = \frac{4}{2}$ or 2

$\frac{1}{4} + \frac{2}{4} =$ _____

$\frac{5}{3} + \frac{2}{3} =$ _____

$\frac{5}{6} + \frac{2}{6} =$ _____

$\frac{1}{12} + \frac{10}{12} =$ _____

$\frac{2}{6} + \frac{3}{6} =$ _____

Subtract the following like fractions:

$\frac{7}{8} - \frac{1}{8} = \frac{6}{8}$ or $\frac{3}{4}$

$\frac{4}{5} - \frac{3}{5} =$ _____

$\frac{10}{2} - \frac{1}{2} =$ _____

$\frac{3}{2} - \frac{1}{2} =$ _____

$\frac{5}{5} - \frac{1}{5} =$ _____

$\frac{3}{4} - \frac{2}{4} =$ _____

Add the following unlike fractions:

$\frac{1}{3} + \frac{1}{2} = \frac{5}{6}$

$\frac{3}{4} + \frac{1}{8} =$ _____

$\frac{1}{5} + \frac{1}{3} =$ _____

$\frac{4}{5} + \frac{1}{10} =$ _____

$\frac{6}{7} + \frac{1}{2} =$ _____

$\frac{4}{10} + \frac{3}{5} =$ _____

Subtract the following unlike fractions:

$\frac{1}{2} - \frac{1}{4} = \frac{1}{4}$

$\frac{7}{8} - \frac{1}{2} =$ _____

$\frac{1}{5} - \frac{1}{10} =$ _____

$\frac{3}{4} - \frac{1}{6} =$ _____

$\frac{4}{5} - \frac{2}{3} =$ _____

$\frac{2}{3} - \frac{2}{6} =$ _____

Multiply the following fractions with whole numbers:

$\frac{1}{2} \times 4 \quad = \quad \boxed{2}$

$\frac{6}{2} \times 8 \quad = \quad \boxed{}$

$\frac{3}{4} \times 16 \quad = \quad \boxed{}$

$\frac{7}{8} \times 64 \quad = \quad \boxed{}$

$\frac{2}{3} \times 2 \quad = \quad \boxed{}$

$\frac{1}{10} \times 5 \quad = \quad \boxed{}$

$\frac{1}{3} \times 9 \quad = \quad \boxed{}$

$\frac{2}{12} \times 24 \quad = \quad \boxed{}$

Multiply the following fractions:

$\frac{3}{4} \times \frac{1}{3} \quad = \quad \boxed{\frac{1}{4}}$

$\frac{1}{4} \times \frac{1}{7} \quad = \quad \boxed{}$

$\frac{3}{4} \times \frac{1}{10} \quad = \quad \boxed{}$

$\frac{6}{18} \times \frac{3}{6} \quad = \quad \boxed{}$

$\frac{6}{2} \times \frac{1}{5} \quad = \quad \boxed{}$

$\frac{3}{8} \times \frac{16}{9} \quad = \quad \boxed{}$

$\frac{1}{5} \times \frac{1}{2} \quad = \quad \boxed{}$

$\frac{6}{8} \times \frac{4}{9} \quad = \quad \boxed{}$

Simplify the following:

$\frac{12}{18} \div 6 \quad = \quad \boxed{\frac{12}{18} \times \frac{1}{6} = \frac{2}{3} \times \frac{1}{6} = \frac{1}{3} \times \frac{1}{3} = \frac{1}{9}}$

$\frac{2}{8} \div 2 \quad = \quad \boxed{}$

$\frac{4}{5} \div 8 \quad = \quad \boxed{}$

$\frac{6}{10} \div 5 \quad = \quad \boxed{}$

$\frac{1}{6} \div \frac{1}{18} \quad = \quad \boxed{}$

Round upto the nearest 10.

31	30	56		62	
47		92		88	
23		67		53	
78		14		9	
36		19		84	

Round upto the nearest 100.

458	500	236		190	
235		323		648	
890		644		526	
921		113		999	
490		783		449	

Round upto the nearest 1000.

5811	6000	3942		1467	
4290		7452		1956	
9119		4134		2841	
4565		8728		3200	
2110		5673		4499	

Solve the following in the space provided below and fill in the blanks:

$4 \times (8 + 3) - 4 =$ 40
$= 4 \times (11) - 4$
$= 44 - 4$
$= 40$

$(64 \div 4) - (27 \div 9)$

$=$ _____

$6 (2 + 7) - 3$

$=$ _____

$45 \div (3 + 2) - 3$

$=$ _____

$4 \times 3 + (7 - 4) - 6$

$=$ _____

$8 \times 5 - (9 \times 2) + 10$

$=$ _____

$7 (7 + 5) - 15$

$=$ _____

$(15 \div 5) (4 \times 2)$

$=$ _____

$6 \div 3 + (8 + 2) - 5$

$=$ _____

$81 \div (6 + 3) \times 2$

$=$ _____

Exercise 87

Complete the table below.

Number	Square	Cube
3	3 × 3 = 9	3 × 3 × 3 = 27
10		
4		
7		
12		
8		
15		
5		
1		
18		
2		
6		
11		
14		
9		
20		
13		
16		

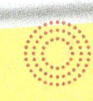

Find the value of a.

$7 \times a = 7$ $a = 1$	$a \times 6 = 18$ _____	$12 \times a = 72$ _____
$3 \times a = 24$ _____	$10 \times a = 50$ _____	$a \times 5 = 70$ _____
$a \times 5 = 45$ _____	$8 \times a = 64$ _____	$9 \times a = 27$ _____
$a \times 11 = 22$ _____	$a \times 7 = 21$ _____	$a \times 6 = 42$ _____

Find the value of b.

$6b \div 2 = 24$ $b = 8$	$35 \div 1b = 7$ _____	$66 \div 3b = 11$ _____
$90 \div 2b = 9$ _____	$42 \div 2b = 7$ _____	$32 \div 2b = 8$ _____
$21 \div 7b = 1$ _____	$3b \div 6 = 13$ _____	$5b \div 5 = 4$ _____
$64 \div 4b = 8$ _____	$85 \div 17b = 5$ _____	$9b \div 2 = 18$ _____

Solve the following:

2^4 $= 2 \times 2 \times 2 \times 2$ $= 16$	2^7 _____
3^5 _____	1^{18} _____
10^4 _____	50^2 _____
4^5 _____	5^5 _____
25^2 _____	2^{10} _____

Find the value of the variables in the following:

If $0.64 = 0.4 \times g$ Then, $g = 1.6$	If $0.96 = 0.8 \times m$ Then, $m =$
If $0.85 = 0.5 \times n$ Then, $n =$	If $0.63 = 0.9 \times h$ Then, $h =$
If $0.81 = 0.9 \times k$ Then, $k =$	If $0.8 = 0.1 \times e$ Then, $e =$
If $0.33 = 1.1 \times d$ Then, $d =$	If $0.28 = 0.07 \times b$ Then, $b =$
If $0.06 = 0.3 \times r$ Then, $r =$	If $0.05 = z \times 0.5$ Then, $k =$
If $0.21 = 0.7 \times c$ Then, $c =$	If $0.72 = a \times 0.8$ Then, $a =$

Complete the magic squares by filling in the empty squares with any number between 1 and 9, in such a way that each row, column and diagonal adds upto the same number.

8	1	6
3	5	7
4	9	2

6		
	5	
8		

4		
	5	
2		

8		
1	5	
	7	

	1	
4		2

	9	2
8		

		8
	5	
7		

4		
	5	7
	1	

Which of the following pairs are parallel lines? Tick the correct ones.

Which of the following pairs of lines are perpendicular to each other? Tick the correct ones.

Carefully analyze the diagram and read the statements given below.

State true or false:

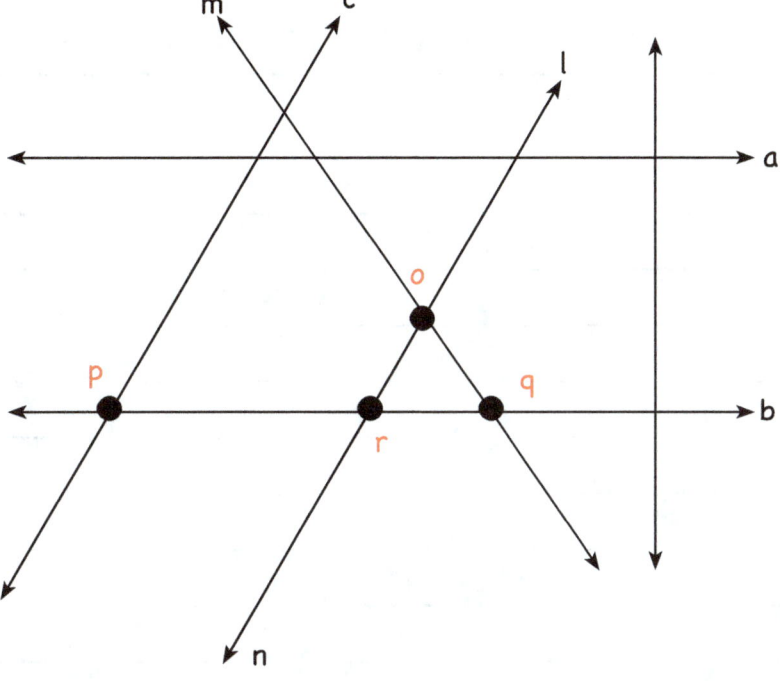

Line l is perpendicular to line a _____

Line n is parallel to line b _____

Line a is parallel to line b _____

Line m and line n intersect each other at o _____

Line m is parallel to line c _____

Line c and line b intersect each other at p _____

Line m is perpendicular to line l _____

Line b is perpendicular to line l _____

Line c is parallel to line n _____

Line n and line b intersect each other at q _____

The graph below shows the number of marks scored by four students in a mathematics test out of 10. Use the information in the graph to answer the questions.

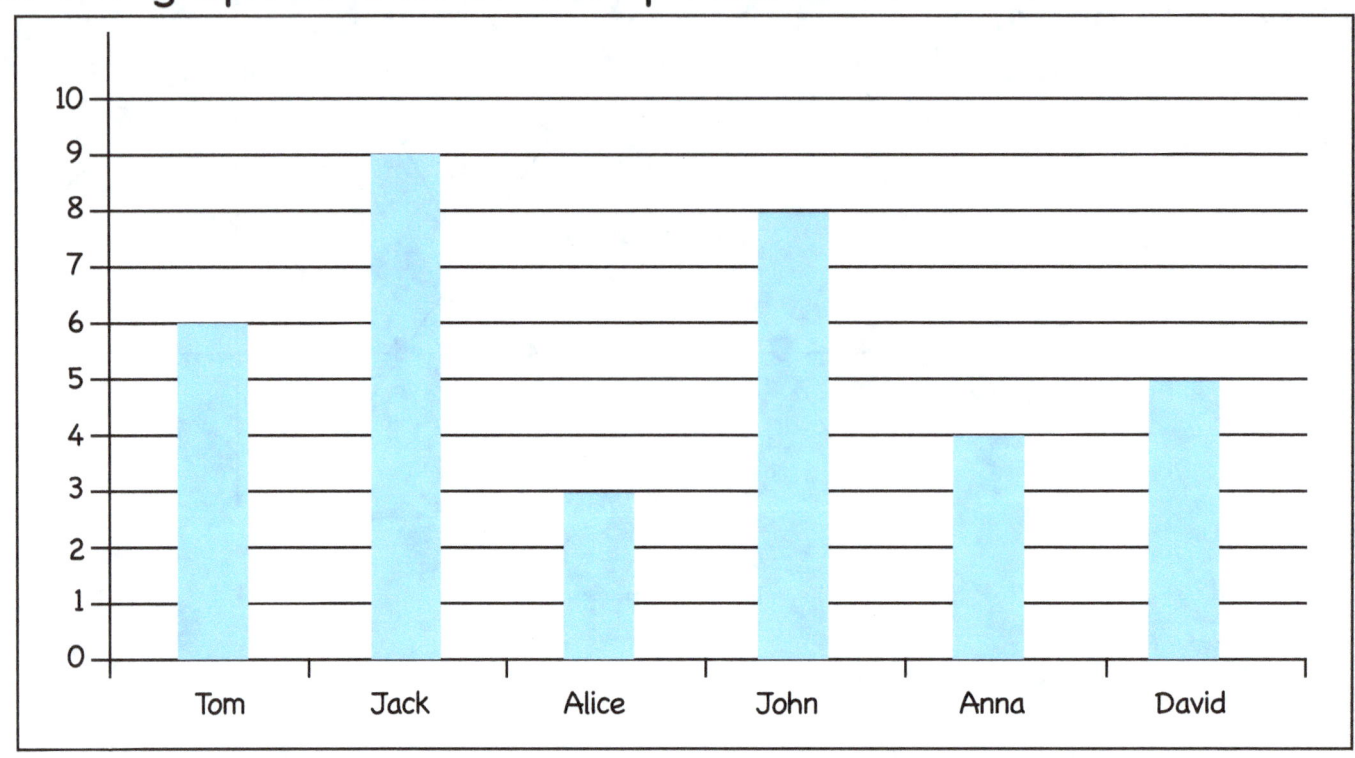

How many marks did Anna score? <u>   4   </u>

What is the lowest score? _____

Who scored the least marks in the test? _____

How many marks did David score less than Jack? _____

How many marks did John and Tom score together? _____

Who scored the highest marks in the test? _____

How many more marks did Tom score than Alice? _____

What is the highest score? _____

How many marks did Tom score? _____

How many marks did David and Anna score together? _____

How many marks did Alice score less than John? _____

Write the coordinates for the points given below.

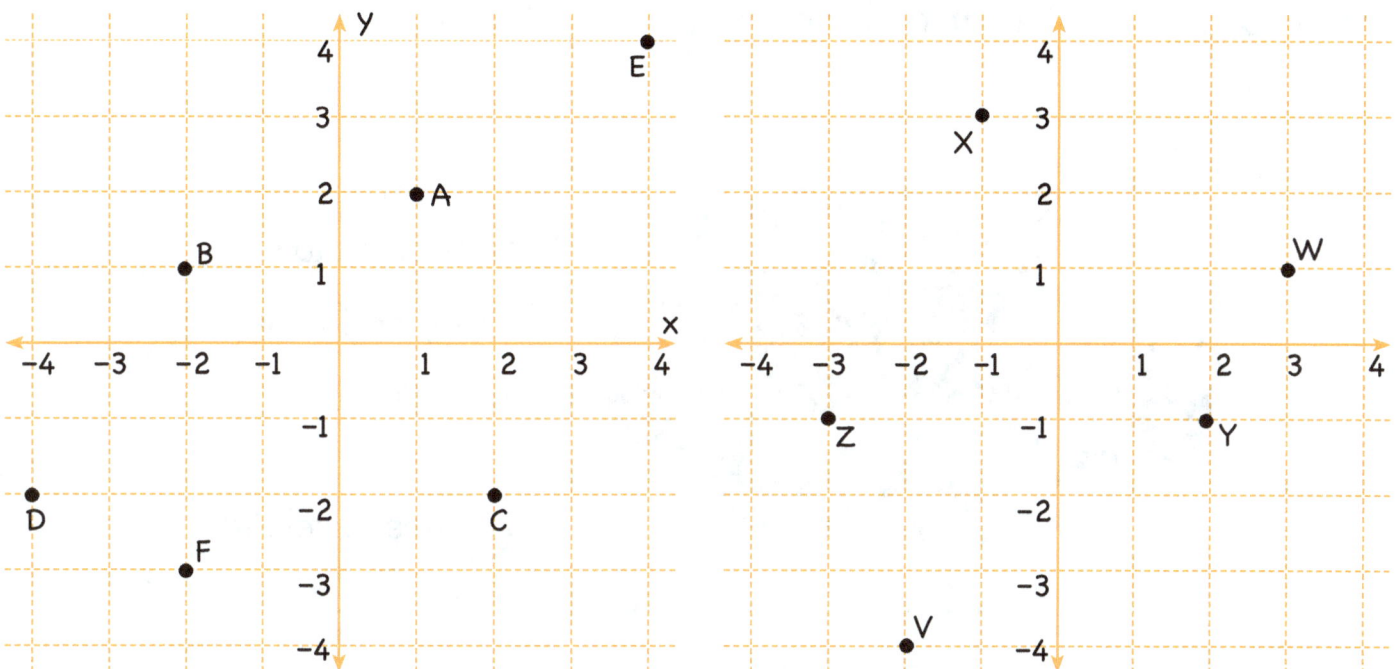

Point	Coordinate	Point	Coordinate
A	(1, 2)	V	
B		W	
C		X	
E		Y	
F		Z	

Write down the next three ordered pairs.

(1, 5), (2, 6), (3, 7), (4 , 8), (5 , 9), (6 , 10)

(6, 3), (8, 4), (10, 5), (___, ___), (___, ___), (___, ___)

(10, 7), (9, 6), (8, 5), (___, ___), (___, ___), (___, ___)

(0, 0), (1, 3), (3, 9), (___, ___), (___, ___), (___, ___)

The pie chart below shows the favourite leisure time activities of about 150 students in a school.

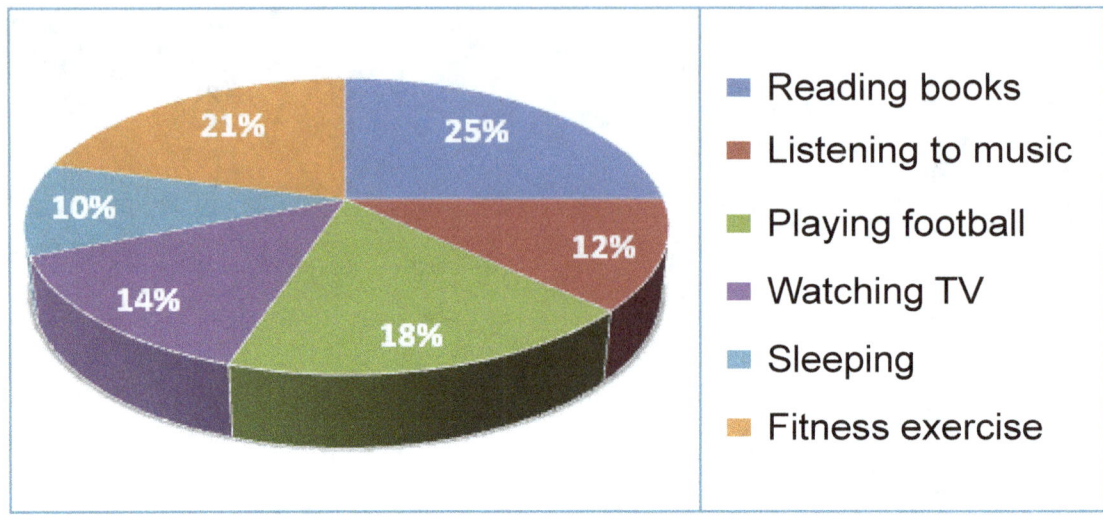

Answer the following questions:

How many students prefer to watch television after school?   <u>21 students</u>

Which activity is preferred by most of the students?   _____

How many students prefer to play football after school?   _____

Which activity is preferred by the least number of students?   _____

How many students prefer to read books after school?   _____

How many more students prefer to exercise than sleep?   _____

How many students like to listen to music?   _____

Calculate profit or loss.

Cost price	Selling price	Profit	Loss
$15.5	$18.9	$3.4	–
$56.75	$35.21		
$96	$49.2		
$10	$4.6		
$38.93	$65.51		
$78.4	$90.2		
$7.50	$5.60		

Calculate the cost price or the selling price.

Cost price	Selling price	Profit	Loss
$4.50	$5.7	$1.20	–
	$33.5	–	$12
$90.25		–	$5.75
$60		$23	–
	$56.1	–	$6.8
		25.36	$1.48
	$16.9	$15.5	–

Solve the following questions.

---

70 toys were bought for $120 and sold at $2 a toy. How much was the profit?

Profit = SP − CP = $140 − $120 = $20

A shopkepper paid $9 for 2 buckets. He sold each of them for $5.5. Calculate the profit.

A shopkeeper sold 2 pairs of shoes for $15 losing $1.6 on each. Calculate the total loss.

A bag of wheat bought for $65.4 is sold for $78.9. Calculate the total profit if 3 such bags are sold.

Jack bought 7 books at $2.2 each and sold all of them for $15. What was the profit/loss?

---

15 m of cloth was bought for $36.9. It was then sold for $3 per metre. Find the total profit or loss.